figure

EYEWITNESS
FOOTBALL

Written by
HUGH HORNBY

Photographed by
ANDY CRAWFORD

1912 football

in association with
THE NATIONAL FOOTBALL MUSEUM

19th-century jersey

1925 Australian international shirt

1905 book cover image

DK | Penguin Random House

RELAUNCH EDITION

DK DELHI
Project editor Antara Moitra
Art editor Revati Anand
DTP designer Pawan Kumar
Senior DTP designer Harish Aggarwal
Senior picture researcher Sumedha Chopra
Jacket designer Tanya Mehrotra
Jackets editorial coordinator Priyanka Sharma
Managing editor Kingshuk Ghoshal
Managing art editor Govind Mittal

DK LONDON
Senior editor Chris Hawkes
Senior art editor Spencer Holbrook
Jacket designer Surabhi Wadhwa   Jacket editor Claire Gell
Jacket design development manager Sophia MTT
Producers, pre-production Andy Hilliard, Marc Staples
Senior producer Angela Graef
Managing editor Francesca Baines
Managing art editor Philip Letsu
Publisher Andrew Macintyre
Associate publishing director Liz Wheeler
Art director Karen Self   Design director Philip Ormerod
Publishing director Jonathan Metcalf

FIRST EDITION
Project editor Louise Pritchard   Art editor Jill Plank
Assistant editor Annabel Blackledge   Assistant art editor Yolanda Belton
Managing art editor Sue Grabham   Senior managing art editor Julia Harris
Production Kate Oliver   Picture research Amanda Russell
DTP designers Andrew O'Brien and Georgia Bryer

This Eyewitness ® Guide has been conceived by
Dorling Kindersley Limited and Editions Gallimard

This edition published in 2018
First published in Great Britain in 2000 by
Dorling Kindersley Limited,
80 Strand, London WC2 0RL

Copyright © 2000, 2004, 2010, 2014, 2018
Dorling Kindersley Limited
A Penguin Random House Company
10 9 8 7 6 5 4 3 2 1
001–308097–June/2018

Text copyright © 2000, 2004, 2010, 2014, 2018
The National Football Museum

A CIP catalogue record for this book is
available from the British Library.

ISBN: 978-0-2413-1768-6

Printed and bound in China

A WORLD OF IDEAS:
SEE ALL THERE IS TO KNOW

www.dk.com

1900s plaster figure

1908 Newcastle shirt

1900s silver match holder

1930s silver hatpin

1920s silver flint lighter

THE REFEREE

Early 20th-century snap card

Shirts from 1890s catalogue

Hungary badge Holland badge Italy badge Brazil badge

Contents

Early 20th-century child's rattle

1930s child's painted rattle

The global game

Football has its roots in ancient China, Europe, and the Americas. People kicked a ball to prepare for war, to honour their gods, or just to entertain themselves. In Europe, ball-kicking games were tests of courage, while in China, they were rituals of grace and skill. The rules of the modern game of football were established in 1863.

An Ashbourne ball

Ashbourne ball
Ashbourne in Derbyshire, England, holds a traditional Shrove Tuesday football game. The Upwards and the Downwards teams try to move the ball through the opposition's "goal" – a gateway at the end of town.

Harrow ball
English boarding schools, including Harrow and Eton, played a crucial role in developing modern football in the early 1800s. Although each school played the game differently, they all produced detailed written rules. These provided the basis for the first official laws.

The Harrow ball was flattened, top and bottom, to allow it to skim across muddy playing fields

Football training
The Chinese were playing a type of football by the 3rd century BCE. A military book of that period refers to *tsu chu*, or "kicking a ball". The game may once have been part of a soldier's training and was later included in ceremonies on the emperor's birthday.

足球

Chinese characters meaning "football"

A gentlemen's game
The game of calcio was played in Italian cities in the 16th and 17th centuries. On festival days, two teams of gentlemen would attempt to force the ball through openings at either end of a city square. Team tactics included formations and the creation of space in which to advance.

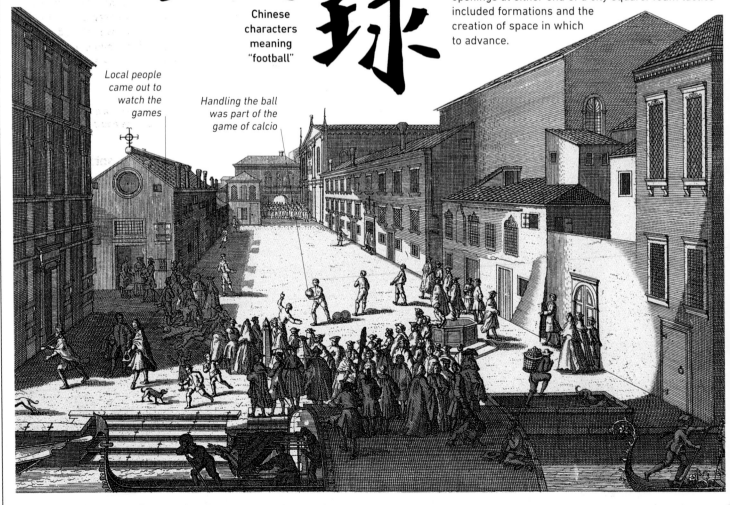

Local people came out to watch the games

Handling the ball was part of the game of calcio

Players wear
an elaborate
costume of silk
and gold brocade

Ball made
from strips
of leather

Men from many different
backgrounds played football

Street games

This early 19th-century cartoon is subtitled "Dustmen, coalmen, gentlemen, and city clerks at murderous if democratic play". It shows the violent "every man for himself" spirit common to street games in Britain at that time. The damage done to property, particularly windows, and the disruption to the lives of other citizens caused many town councils to ban football – without much success.

Ancient ritual

The Japanese game of *kemari* probably developed in the 7th century from an ancient Chinese football game, after contact was made between the two countries. Unlike the chaotic early football brawls of Europe, it involved many rituals and was played as part of a ceremony. The game is still played by keeping a ball in the air inside a small court.

Kemari is a game of balance and skill

Football writing

Football has been a literary subject for as long as the game has been played. The first book on football is *Discourse on Calcio* by Italian Giovanni da Bardi, published in 1580. As football became popular in the early 20th century, many children's books were published, including *The School Across the Road* by Desmond Coke.

**16th-century
discourse on
football**

**18th-century
anthology**

**The children's
book *The School
Across the Road***

*Colour prints appear
throughout the book*

*Image from
a 9th-century
watercolour
on silk*

History of football

The global game was developed in England and Scotland in the 19th century. Former pupils of English boarding schools produced the first common set of rules and formed the Football Association (FA) in 1863. British merchants and engineers took the game overseas, so people from other countries began to play football.

Celebrity player
The first footballers were amateurs. C B Fry, who played for the Corinthians in the 1890s, was one of the first football celebrities. He also held the world long-jump record.

Exhibitionism
In the early 20th century, British teams toured the world, introducing football to other nations by playing exhibition matches. This shield was presented to the Islington Corinthians in Japan, in 1937.

Kinnaird played in nine of the first 12 FA Cup finals

Arnold Kirke Smith's cap

The English Three Lions motif was first used in 1872

Arnold Kirke Smith's England shirt

The shirt is made of closely woven wool

The first international
In November 1872, Scotland played England on a cricket field in Glasgow in the first-ever international match. About 2,000 spectators watched a 0–0 draw. This shirt and cap were worn by Arnold Kirke Smith from Oxford University, who was a member of the English team.

Modern rules
Lord Kinnaird was president of the Football Association from 1890 to 1923, and was one of the amateurs who shaped the rules of the modern game.

Talented teams
The English Football League began in 1888. Its 12-team fixture programme was inspired by US baseball. This 1893 painting by Thomas Hemy shows Aston Villa and Sunderland.

The unruly game

The first French football league, set up in 1894, was dominated by teams of Scottish emigrants, such as the White Rovers and Standard AC. French satirists were quick to refer to the game's reputation for unruliness. This 1900s French magazine, *Le Monde Comique*, reflects this attitude towards the game.

Bystanders often got caught up in the boisterous action

Cover illustration entitled *"Les Plaisirs du Dimanche"* ("Sunday Pleasures")

In reality, women's kit was far less figure-hugging

A ball of exaggerated size

Ladies first

Women's football started at the end of the 19th century. Teams such as the British Ladies Club attracted large crowds. During World War I, men's and women's teams played against each other for charity. The first Women's World Cup was held in China in 1991 and was won by the USA.

FIFA badge

Forming FIFA

By 1904, many European countries had their own administrators. They formed the world governing body, FIFA (Fédération Internationale de Football Associations). Today, it has more than 200 members.

This 1900s plaster figure is wearing shin-pads that were typical of that time

Image of a football match played in Uganda, Africa

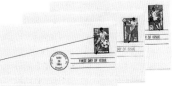

Each stamp shows a different US player

US stamps produced for the 1994 World Cup

Out of Africa

Football spread through Africa. South Africa, with its European populations, sent a touring party to South America in 1906. In 1923, Egypt became the first African country to join FIFA. In 2010, South Africa became the first African country to host the World Cup finals.

Soccer

Soccer is a popular youth sport in the USA. The 1994 World Cup finals held in the USA provided a boost for Major League Soccer, which is bringing professional games to a new audience.

Laws of the game

Football's success is partly due to its simple laws. Rules governing foul play, equipment, and restarts have survived the test of time. Stoppages in the game can be avoided if the referee uses the advantage rule, allowing play to continue after a foul if the right team has the ball. For the offside rule, the assistant referees decide if an attacker has strayed beyond the second-last defender when the ball is played forward by a team-mate.

Stand back
This throw-in is illegal. The ball is held correctly in both hands, but the feet are over the line.

The penalty spot is 12 yd (11 m) from the goal-line

Before the crossbar was introduced, tape was stretched between the goal posts

Goal kicks must be taken from within the 6-yd (5.5-m) box

Players must not cross the halfway line until the ball is kicked off

Penalty
In 1891, penalties were introduced to punish foul play, such as tripping, pushing, or handball within 12 yd (11 m) of the goal. A player shoots from the penalty spot to beat the keeper. If the ball hits the post or bar the penalty taker cannot play it until another player touches it.

Free kick
There are two types of free kick – direct and indirect. In an indirect free kick, awarded after an infringement of a law, the ball must be touched by two players before a goal is scored. Direct free kicks are given after fouls and the taker may score immediately.

Corner
A corner kick is taken when the defending team puts the ball out of play behind their own goal-line. Corner kicks are good goal-scoring opportunities. The ball is placed within the quadrant – a quarter circle with a radius of 1 yd (1 m) in the corner of the pitch.

Faking fouls
Amateur footballers in the 19th century believed all fouls were accidental and would have been horrified by the "professional foul", a deliberate offence to prevent an attack. The modern game has many deliberate fouls. Some players fake being fouled to win a free kick.

When a penalty is taken, only the taker is allowed inside the "D"

Charge!

The 1958 English FA Cup final between Manchester United and Bolton Wanderers featured a disputed goal by Bolton's Nat Lofthouse. He charged United goalkeeper Harry Gregg over the line as he caught the ball. Referees would now call it a foul.

Players from the defending team must stay out of the 10-yd (9-m) circle before kick-off

Players cannot be offside in their own half of the pitch

The 6-yd (5.5-m) box was semi-circular until 1902. The penalty box was introduced in the same year

Assistant referees patrol opposite sides of the field and cover one half each to signal throw-ins and flag for offside

Law and order

There are 17 main football laws. The field of play must be rectangular and, for a full-size pitch, from 110 to 120 yd (100.5 to 110 m) long and from 70 to 80 yd (64 to 73 m) wide. There should be 11 players per side. The duration of play is 90 minutes, in two halves of 45 minutes each.

Permanent markers

In the mid-19th century, before lines were marked on the pitch, flags were used to decide whether the ball was out of play. Today, a corner flag has to be at least 1.5 m (5 ft) high to avoid the risk of players being impaled.

Goal nets, patented by Brodies of Liverpool, England, in 1891, were first used in 1892 to settle disputes over whether a ball had entered the goal

11

The referee

Early amateur players wanted officials to encourage fair play. Each team had an umpire. Players had to raise an arm and appeal against a foul; otherwise, play continued. The rise of professional football in the 1880s made it harder for umpires to be neutral. A referee was introduced to settle disputes. In 1891, the referee moved onto the pitch and the umpires became linesmen. They are now officially known as assistant referees.

Early 20th-century snap card caricature of a referee

Your number's up
The assistant referee controls the entrance of substitutes to the field and checks their boot studs. At top levels, a fourth official uses an illuminated board to indicate the shirt number of the substitute and the player being replaced, and confirm how much stoppage time there will be in each half.

Classic black
This is the classic referee's uniform, all-black with white cuffs and collar. This kit is from the 1970s, and is similar to all those worn between the phasing out of the blazer in the 1940s and the introduction of other colours in the 1990s. The bulky jackets of the early 1900s were replaced by less constricting shirts to encourage the officials to keep up with play on the pitch.

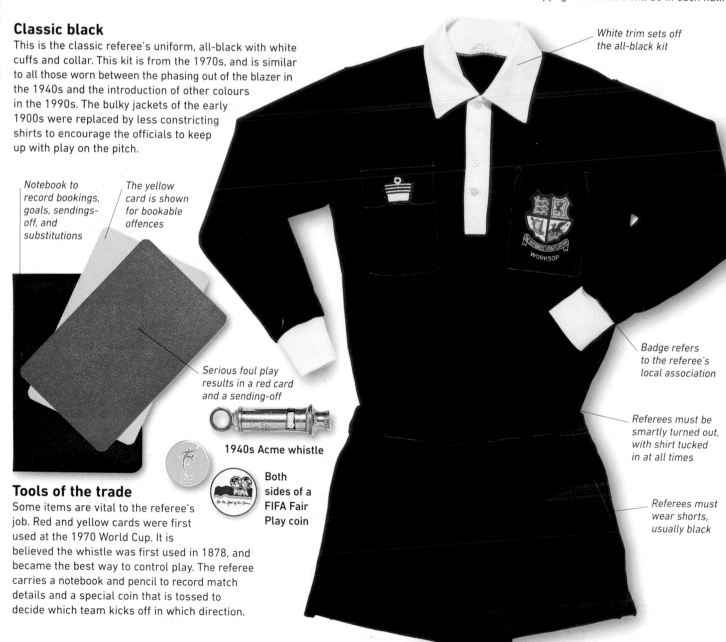

White trim sets off the all-black kit

Notebook to record bookings, goals, sendings-off, and substitutions

The yellow card is shown for bookable offences

Serious foul play results in a red card and a sending-off

1940s Acme whistle

Both sides of a FIFA Fair Play coin

Badge refers to the referee's local association

Referees must be smartly turned out, with shirt tucked in at all times

Referees must wear shorts, usually black

Tools of the trade
Some items are vital to the referee's job. Red and yellow cards were first used at the 1970 World Cup. It is believed the whistle was first used in 1878, and became the best way to control play. The referee carries a notebook and pencil to record match details and a special coin that is tossed to decide which team kicks off in which direction.

You're booked

Bookings used to be given only once or twice a match and sendings-off were rare, but FIFA now insist that referees are strict. As a result, teams regularly have to play with 10 team members, or even fewer.

A whistle is blown to indicate the start or restart of play, or to stop play due to a foul or injury

A red card is shown when a player has committed two bookable offences, although players can be shown a red card for a serious offence, such as a dangerous tackle

JANKULOVSKI 18

DIADORA

Referees have to be fit to keep up with play on the pitch

Former USSR

Australia

New Zealand

Bangladesh

Iceland

Portugal

USA

Colombia

Italy

World-class referees

These badges are produced by referees' associations around the world. Referees are motivated by the prospect of officiating at top-class games. World Cup matches are controlled by officials from all countries affiliated to FIFA.

LINESMAN FIFA 92

LINESWOMAN FIFA 95

Official FIFA badges for sewing on the officials' shirts

Men and women officiate at top-level matches

Touchline helpers

The first linesmen waved a handkerchief to alert the referee. Assistant referees now wave a flag for offside, for when the ball is out of play, and for any infringement.

The first referees wore plus-two trousers

Blazer with pockets for a stopwatch and notebook

How to be a referee

This illustration from the cover of a 1906 book entitled *How to be a Referee* shows the typical referee's clothing of that period. After taking a qualifying exam, referees usually start out at amateur level. They are assessed regularly to ensure high standards. Today's top referees are professionals.

The pitch

At the start of a season, the pitch is smooth and green. But it soon becomes muddy and uneven, especially if cold, wet weather sets in. Ground staff keep pitches in top condition with new species of grass and good drainage. Some wealthy clubs lay a completely new pitch between matches, but amateur players make do with any muddy or frozen surface.

This Samuel Brandão painting shows football being played on bare earth in Rio de Janeiro, Brazil

Patterns can be made when mowing the pitch

Streets ahead

In the days before busy traffic, street football was popular. Children learned ball control and dribbling skills in confined spaces. They often used clothes as goalposts.

Ground staff preparing for a match during the 1953 English season

Jean-Pierre Papin playing for AC Milan, Italy, on a snowy pitch

Playing in snow

In snow, the ball and pitch markings are hard to see and the ground is slippery. If the markings are swept clear and the pitch is soft for studs, play can carry on.

Hot stuff

In colder countries, various methods have been tried to prevent football pitches from freezing. Undersoil heating was first installed at Everton, England, in 1958. In the past, ground staff put straw down as insulation and lit fires in braziers to lift the air temperature.

Slopes and shade

Modern pitches, such as Brighton and Hove Albion's (above), are usually laid with a camber, which means they slope slightly down from the centre circle to the touchlines to drain water away. With large stands, less air and light reach the grass, stunting its growth. This has been a problem at some stadiums.

Pampering the pitch

Modern pitch maintenance is a full-time job. In summer, the grass is mowed, watered, and fed regularly. During the close season, work is done to repair holes and worn patches in the turf. New grass types have been created that grow better in the shade of tall stands.

The surface is made to mimic grass

Fibres are woven together to form a carpet

Artificial grass viewed from the side, above, and underneath

Grass is kept long to encourage deep rooting *Layer of topsoil nourishes the grass* *Heating pipes are laid in grids* *Layers of sand and gravel allow water to filter away*

The base of the pitch is composed of large pieces of stone *Drainage pipes carry away water*

Model of a section through a pitch

Better than the real thing?

Artificial pitches are made from synthetic turf laid on a shock-absorbent pad. They are more hard-wearing than grass pitches and are unaffected by rain or ice. However, many players feel they increase the risk of injury. Today, most top clubs prefer hybrid pitches, which have artificial grass woven in real grass.

Saturation point

Rainwater is the greatest threat to pitch condition. Built-in drainage is an important part of pitch construction. Pipes and materials chosen for their draining qualities are laid under grass. Lots of sand is mixed into the topsoil to make it less absorbent and less waterlogged. Even a well-cared-for pitch may become saturated.

Football skills

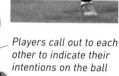

Each position on the field is associated with specific tasks. Defenders must tackle opponents to claim the ball, midfielders must pass the ball accurately to their team-mates, and strikers must shoot and score goals. Professional players master and perfect a range of skills in their training routines.

Early 20th-century button showing a man heading the ball

Control freak

The best players always bring the ball under control. For high passes, they keep their eye on the ball and use their chest, stomach, head, or, like Wayne Rooney here, their thighs to stun the ball.

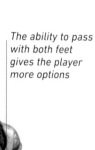

Players call out to each other to indicate their intentions on the ball

Tackle talk

Players try to take the ball from another player by tackling. Germany's Mats Hummels is one of the finest tacklers in modern football. He shows the anticipation and timing that are essential to avoid committing a foul. Referees punish players if they make a physical challenge from behind or if they make contact with a player instead of the ball.

Pass mark

Moving the ball fast between players stretches a defence. Accurate passing is the hallmark of all successful teams. Former Barcelona player Xavi could pass the ball into space even when he was tightly marked.

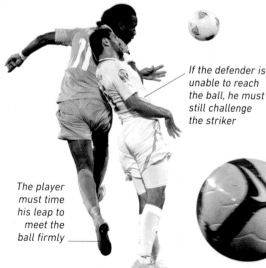

If the defender is unable to reach the ball, he must still challenge the striker

All parts of the foot are used to manipulate the ball in the desired direction

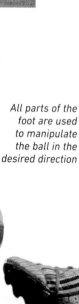

The player must time his leap to meet the ball firmly

The ability to pass with both feet gives the player more options

Heads up!

Headers can be defensive or attacking. Defenders try to gain distance when they clear a ball from the goal area. Attackers need power and accuracy to head in a goal. Ivory Coast striker Didier Drogba uses his height to beat the opponent and head the ball.

Winging it

Crosses, or passes in from the wings, result in more goals than any other angle of attack. Players who can put the ball over with pace and accuracy are valuable to a team. Portugal and Real Madrid winger Cristiano Ronaldo arguably takes the greatest free kicks. He can put great power behind the ball while applying curve or dip. He plants his left foot alongside the ball and uses his arms to maintain balance before driving his right foot through the ball. The way his foot strikes the ball dictates the dip or curl.

Keeping the head still improves accuracy

Extending the arms assists with balance

The player can pretend to go in one direction before going in the other

Keeping body weight over the ball makes it easier to cross with power

Downtown dribbler

When a player runs with the ball at his or her feet, it is called dribbling. Brazilian star Ronaldinho, who learned his football on the streets of Porto Alegre, is proof that dribbling can cause problems for the opposition. Good balance and concentration help a dribbler change direction quickly and ride tackles.

The foot turns in as it passes through the ball to make it swerve

Keeping the head down and looking at the ball rather than the goal helps to ensure clean contact

The bicycle kick is even harder to execute if the ball is moving across the player

Going for goal

When shooting, forwards need the accuracy to find the corner of the net as well as the power to blast the ball past the goalkeeper. Edinson Cavani of Uruguay is one of the most reliable goalscorers in world football.

The left leg is firmly planted to allow the body to make the best shape for the cross

Bicycle kick

The bicycle kick was first demonstrated in the 1930s by Brazilian forward Leônidas. With their back to the goal, strikers throw their legs up in the air and kick the ball while falling backwards. This tactic can catch the goalkeeper by surprise. This model of Italian striker Roberto Baggio shows the ideal body position.

A higher jump allows the player to keep the ball down below the crossbar

A 1900s match holder showing a goalkeeper punching clear

Goalkeepers

As the last line of defence, a goalkeeper knows that a single mistake can cost the team victory. Goalkeeping can be a lonely job. It involves different skills and more time with nothing to do. The necessity of having both a physical presence and great agility means that goalkeepers have to train as hard as other players, but the reward can be a much longer career.

Clothes

Until 1909, goalkeepers were distinguishable only by their cap, making it difficult for the referee to judge who, in a goalmouth scramble, was handling the ball. From 1909 to the early 1990s, they wore a shirt of a single plain colour that was different from the shirts worn by the rest of their team. A rule was made forbidding short sleeves, which has now been relaxed.

Good save
This 1950 comic cover shows the save that is considered the easiest – from a shot straight to the midriff. It also hints at the spectacular action in which goalkeepers are regularly involved, such as when they have to fly through the air to tip the ball away. Modern strikers can make the ball swerve suddenly, so goalkeepers must keep their bodies in line with the ball.

The ball should be punched out towards the wing

Catch it
Punching the ball away from the danger area has always been popular among European and South American goalkeepers. The keeper on this 1900 book cover is trying to punch the ball clear. Modern referees rarely allow keepers to be challenged when they are trying to catch the ball.

Keepers' colours
Patterns in football shirts have traditionally been limited to stripes and hoops, but since the rules on goalkeepers' clothes were relaxed, every combination of colours seems to have been tried. Not all of them have been easy on the eye, although fluorescent designs are easy for defenders to see.

Flexible plastic ribs reinforce each finger

Modern gloves help prevent injuries such as a broken finger

Eire shirt
This shirt was worn by Alan Kelly for the Republic of Ireland. He made 47 appearances, the first in 1957 and the last in 1973. Yellow shirts were once a common sight in international matches.

The shamrock, symbol of Ireland

Goalie's gloves
Until the 1970s, cotton gloves were worn only when it was wet. Modern keepers always wear gloves. Various coatings and pads are used to increase the gloves' grip.

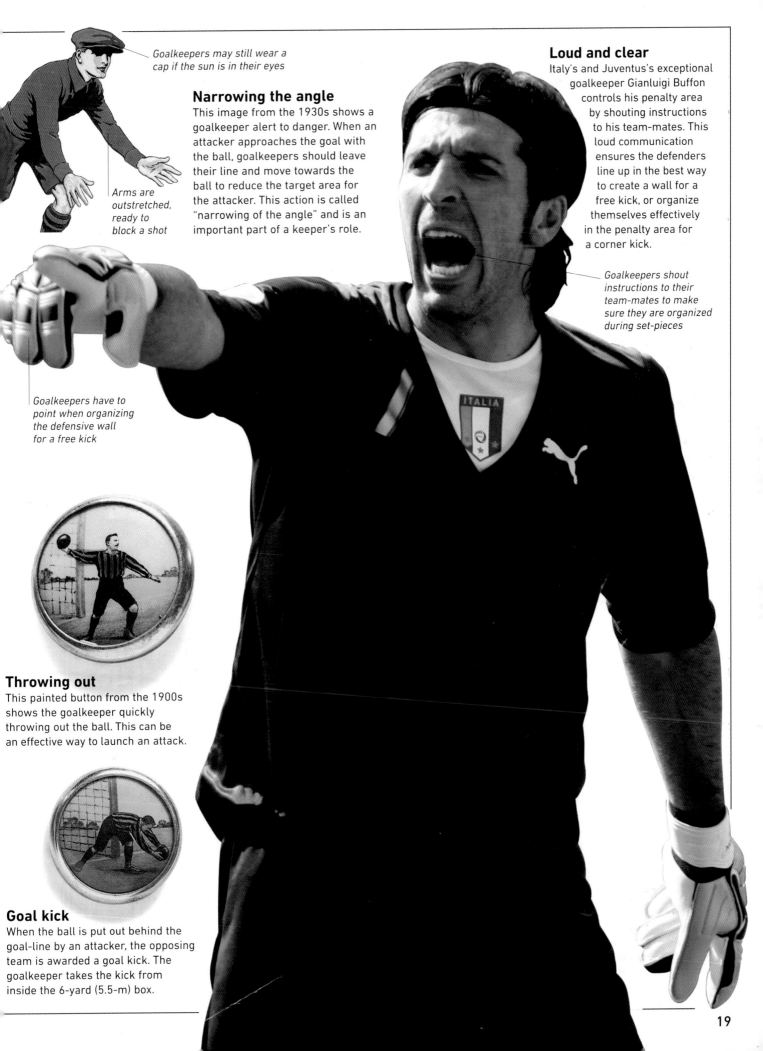

Goalkeepers may still wear a cap if the sun is in their eyes

Arms are outstretched, ready to block a shot

Narrowing the angle

This image from the 1930s shows a goalkeeper alert to danger. When an attacker approaches the goal with the ball, goalkeepers should leave their line and move towards the ball to reduce the target area for the attacker. This action is called "narrowing of the angle" and is an important part of a keeper's role.

Loud and clear

Italy's and Juventus's exceptional goalkeeper Gianluigi Buffon controls his penalty area by shouting instructions to his team-mates. This loud communication ensures the defenders line up in the best way to create a wall for a free kick, or organize themselves effectively in the penalty area for a corner kick.

Goalkeepers shout instructions to their team-mates to make sure they are organized during set-pieces

Goalkeepers have to point when organizing the defensive wall for a free kick

Throwing out

This painted button from the 1900s shows the goalkeeper quickly throwing out the ball. This can be an effective way to launch an attack.

Goal kick

When the ball is put out behind the goal-line by an attacker, the opposing team is awarded a goal kick. The goalkeeper takes the kick from inside the 6-yard (5.5-m) box.

Tactics

Coaches and managers outwit the opposition by keeping their tactics secret until the match. Since football began, teams have lined up in different formations. Early players had the skills needed for a particular position on the field. The pace of today's game demands that players adapt to play in almost any position.

Old Arabic print of team formations

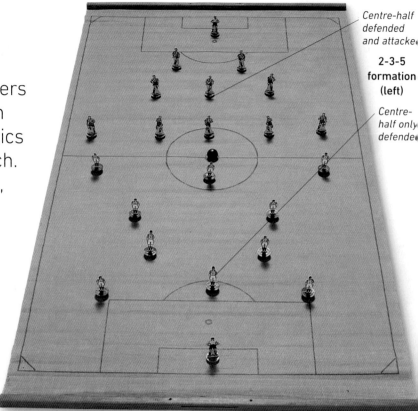

Centre-half defended and attacked

2-3-5 formation (left)

Centre-half only defended

Germany won the 2014 World Cup with a back four

W-M formation (right)

Wingers have been replaced by midfielders who can also defend

4-4-2 formation (right)

One forward often plays "in the hole" behind the other

Wing-backs are responsible for providing attacking width

Sweeper system (left)

Sweeper must be creative and pass accurately

In good form

The 2-3-5 formation dominated tactics until the 1930s. Each player had a specific place on the pitch. Herbert Chapman of Arsenal, England, was the first manager to position the centre-half and inside-forwards deeper to create the W-M formation.

Game plan

Software companies have created computer programs to enable managers to plan their tactics on-screen. This 4-3-3 formation is now one of the most common in football.

Clean sweep

Modern formations are varied, but the 4-4-2 is one of the most popular. The four defenders are not expected to push forwards and the four midfielders sometimes switch to a diamond shape. The sweeper system frees one player from marking duties to act as cover.

Packed defence

Denying the opposition forward space is vital and certain players may be singled out for man-to-man marking. It is said that the best teams are built from the back, with a strong defence providing a springboard for attack. Here, Paris FC defenders are surrounding a striker.

The attacker is trapped

The defenders are physically blocking in the attacker

The forward cannot go "one on one" with the goalkeeper

Offside origins

The first offside law, in 1866, stated that three defenders, including the goalkeeper, had to be between the attacker and the goal when the ball was played forwards by a team-mate. By 1920, fewer goals went in because attackers still had to beat the last outfield defender.

Player is onside

Offside updated

In 1925, FIFA amended the offside law so that only two players had to be between the attacker and the goal. Far more goals were scored. The offside rule is basically unchanged today. Here, the midfielder is about to pass the ball to the forward. This player is still onside and will have only the goalkeeper to beat.

Player is offside

Offside trap

Teams without a sweeper can still use an offside trap. As the midfielder goes to pass the ball forwards, the defenders advance up the field in a line, leaving the forward offside when the ball is played. William McCracken of Newcastle, England, perfected this tactic in the years before World War I.

No substitute

FIFA introduced substitutions in 1923 if a player was injured. Injuries were faked to let coaches make tactical changes, so it was accepted that one player could be freely replaced. Today, the number of substitutions allowed is three per team.

Be prepared

Javier Zanetti's goal for Argentina against England at the 1998 World Cup in France was an example of a brilliant well-rehearsed routine. Many goals are scored from set-pieces – match situations that a team practises before a game.

Injury time

A professional footballer's job involves far more than playing matches. Training, fitness, and recovery from injuries are concerns for the modern player. Advances in medicine mean more injuries can now be successfully treated. Physiotherapy, nutrition, and even psychology are all part of the routine at big clubs today.

Mr Black the footballer from a Happy Families card game

4 - CAMPIONATI MONDIALI DI CALCIO

NOVO: il brodo ricco di 12 saporiti ingredienti

Vital edge
Manager Vittorio Pozzo led Italy to victory in the World Cup in 1934 and 1938. He rated physical fitness and trained his team hard to give them more stamina. This paid off in extra time in the 1934 final against Czechoslovakia when Italy scored the winner.

Fighting fit
Medicine balls like this were used in football training for many decades. They are very heavy, so throwing them improves stamina and builds muscle bulk. Gym equipment, training programmes, and resistance machines are now commonly used. Strength and fitness are essential to success because top players have to play as many as 70 games per season.

Up and down
Modern players know the importance of warming up before a game. The risk of muscle tears and strains is significantly reduced if the muscles are warm and loose. Many teams "warm down" after a match to relax their muscles before resting them.

The stretcher is carried by two wooden poles

A pillow is built into the stretcher

A piece of canvas supports the injured player

Getting carried away
This stretcher was used in the 1920s. In those days, if the stretcher was brought out onto the pitch, the crowd knew that a player was seriously injured. Today, players who are injured have to leave the pitch after treatment, and if fit to resume, are only allowed to rejoin play a few moments later. In many countries, motorized buggies or carts have taken the place of traditional stretchers.

As if by magic
The "magic" sponge has a special place in football folklore. Spectators have often wondered how a rub down with a sponge and cold water could result in a player's swift recovery from an injury. Today, the team physiotherapist, rather than the trainer, treats players for injury problems on the pitch and off it. Physiotherapists are fully qualified to give sophisticated treatment to injured players.

The sponge is still used in amateur games

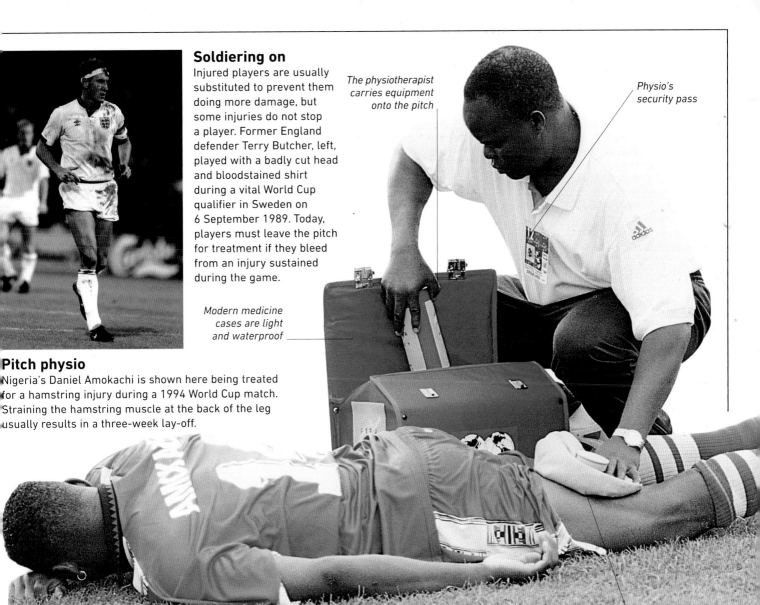

Soldiering on

Injured players are usually substituted to prevent them doing more damage, but some injuries do not stop a player. Former England defender Terry Butcher, left, played with a badly cut head and bloodstained shirt during a vital World Cup qualifier in Sweden on 6 September 1989. Today, players must leave the pitch for treatment if they bleed from an injury sustained during the game.

The physiotherapist carries equipment onto the pitch

Physio's security pass

Modern medicine cases are light and waterproof

Pitch physio

Nigeria's Daniel Amokachi is shown here being treated for a hamstring injury during a 1994 World Cup match. Straining the hamstring muscle at the back of the leg usually results in a three-week lay-off.

Ice is applied to the injury to reduce inflammation

The bag is made of leather

Lotions and potions

This medicine bag belonged to Ramsgate FC in the early 20th century. They were a non-league team from Kent in England. The bottles would have contained lotions to warm muscles, pour on grazes, or reduce pain. Professional clubs are now required to have a doctor at every game to deal with the most serious injuries.

The trainer's medicines sometimes included chloroform to sedate a badly injured player

Footalls

An 1890s brass travelling inkwell in the shape of a football

The game of football can be played without any special equipment. Children can kick around a tin can or bound-up rags. Centuries ago, people found that an animal's bladder could be inflated and knotted to make a light, bouncy ball. A bladder did not last long when kicked, so people protected bladders in a shell of animal skin cured to turn it into leather. This design is still used today, but with modern, synthetic materials.

Heavy going

Balls of the 1870s were often formed by stitching together eight segments of leather, the ends of which were secured by a central disc. The leather was unprotected and could absorb water on wet days, so the ball increased in weight. Heading the ball could be dangerous, and so this technique was not often used in those days. The dribbling game was the popular style and the heavy ball was suitable for this style of play.

Manufacturers' names were first stencilled on balls in about 1900

The lace for tightening the case stands proud

Interlocking panels of leather

Sections of leather sewn together

Tool for lacing the ball tightly

Copper stencil

Made to measure

This ball was used in March 1912, in a match between Wales and England. Made from a pig's bladder wrapped in cowhide, it is typical of the balls used for most of the 20th century. The outside shell was laced up. The size and weight of footballs were standardized for the first FA Challenge Cup competition in 1872, but the balls still absorbed water and lost shape.

The colours are based on the French flag

Brand name marked on the ball with a stencil

World Cup colours

The first World Cup balls to have a colour other than black were used at the 1998 World Cup in France. They had a synthetic coating to make them waterproof and a foam layer between the latex bladder and polyester skin. This let players pass and shoot quickly. Like 75 per cent of footballs, they were made in the Sialkot region of Pakistan.

Heading for trouble

Balls like this were used at the 1966 World Cup when the design had hardly changed in 50 years. The leather case was lined, a 1940s development to improve durability. The outside was painted with a pigment to repel water from a rain-soaked pitch. Manufacturers had not found an alternative to lacing up the ball, so players risked injury when heading the ball.

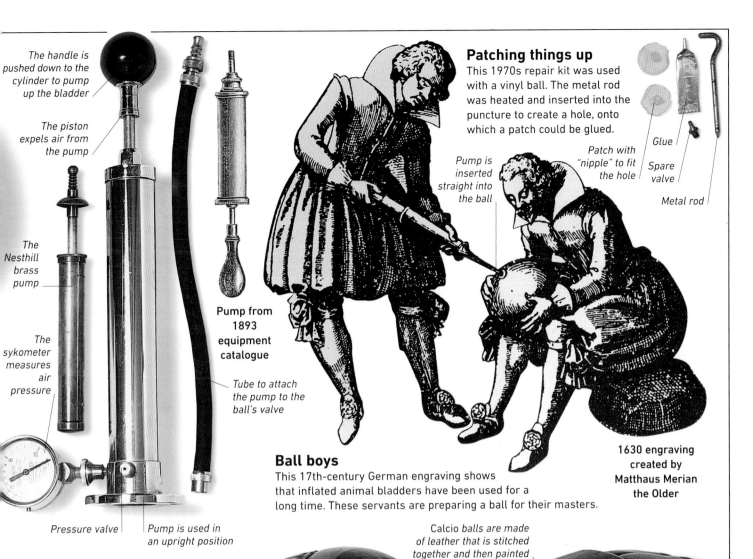

The handle is pushed down to the cylinder to pump up the bladder

The piston expels air from the pump

The Nesthill brass pump

The sykometer measures air pressure

Pressure valve

Pump is used in an upright position

Pump from 1893 equipment catalogue

Tube to attach the pump to the ball's valve

Patching things up
This 1970s repair kit was used with a vinyl ball. The metal rod was heated and inserted into the puncture to create a hole, onto which a patch could be glued.

Pump is inserted straight into the ball

Glue

Patch with "nipple" to fit the hole

Spare valve

Metal rod

Ball boys
This 17th-century German engraving shows that inflated animal bladders have been used for a long time. These servants are preparing a ball for their masters.

1630 engraving created by Matthaus Merian the Older

Full of air
Over time, air escaped from a football's bladder and a pump was used to reinflate it. Air pressure in a bladder could be increased to improve the bounce. If a bladder was pumped too high it could burst, so some pumps came with their own pressure gauge. These pumps date from the 1890s.

Two colours make the Orkney ball flash in the air

Calcio balls are made of leather that is stitched together and then painted

Alternative balls
Several different football games are played around the world. They each use a ball specific to that game. Some football games have existed for centuries. The balls may have features connected to a ceremonial aspect of the game, and involve decoration, or they are designed to withstand very harsh treatment.

Shaping up
American football was based on kicking a ball. As throwing became a feature, the present ball shape evolved. The small ball can be gripped firmly, making it easier to pass accurately.

Built to last
In the Scottish Orkney Isles, a football game is played in the streets every New Year. The ball is very heavy and stuffed with cork. This helps it to last for several hours of play and makes it float on water – a useful feature as a team can score a goal by throwing the ball into the sea.

Made to match
Calcio, first played in Italy in the 16th century, was reintroduced to Florence in 1930. The game is played by teams of 27 a side, all wearing medieval clothes and armour. Red, green, and white balls match the costumes. As *Calcio* balls are small, it is easier for players to pick them up and throw them.

Boots

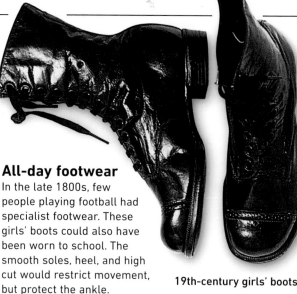

Of all football equipment, boots have changed the most in the last 100 years. As the most expensive item of kit, boots are unaffordable for many people who play in bare feet. The fast sport we see today would be impossible if football players had to use the heavy, painful boots worn until the 1930s. In the first World Cup tournaments in the 1930s, South American teams wore lighter low-cut boots, starting the trend towards the modern, high-tech boot.

A 1950s painting of football boots called *Christopher's Boots,* by Doris Brand

All-day footwear

In the late 1800s, few people playing football had specialist footwear. These girls' boots could also have been worn to school. The smooth soles, heel, and high cut would restrict movement, but protect the ankle.

19th-century girls' boots

1920s children's boots

A "kick around" is a popular pastime with children

Made for the job

By the 1920s, football boots like the "Manfield Hotspur" were being mass-produced for footballers of all ages. Children's boots were designed just like adults', with reinforced toecaps and heels, some ankle protection, and leather studs. Social conditions at the time, though, meant that most working-class families could not afford such equipment and, if they could, they would have handed down boots from one child to another.

Extra foot support

Cotton laces

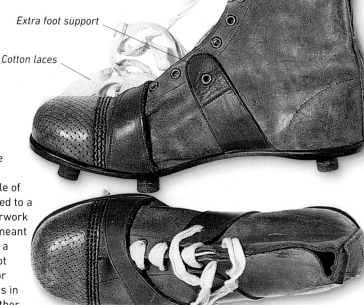

Studless boots

A 19th-century gentleman footballer wore studless boots, which would not have allowed for sharp turns or long passing. However, they were practical enough for the type of dribbling game favoured by the great English amateur teams. This style of play was dictated by the confined spaces used for football practice at many British public schools. Boots like these would have doubled in weight when wet.

Boots in the bath

In 1910, these boots were marketed as "Cup Final Specials", an early example of a football product being tied to a famous match. The wickerwork pattern on the toes was meant to help ball control – also a major part of modern boot design. It was common for players to wear new boots in the bath to soften the leather.

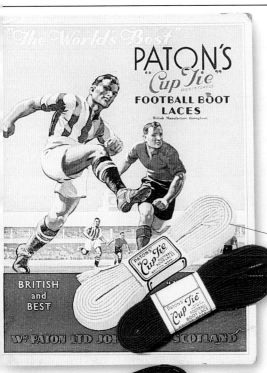

PATON'S "Cup Tie" (REGISTERED)
FOOTBALL BOOT LACES
British Manufacture throughout.

BRITISH and BEST

Wᵐ PATON LTD JOH... SCOTLAND

Lots of laces

Paton's bootlaces, in various colours, were widely used from the 1930s onwards. There was a constant demand for replacements because repeated soaking during matches, followed by drying out, caused the early cotton laces to perish and eventually snap.

White laces were common in the 1930s

Sponsorship deals

Over the last 50 years, star players, such as Neymar of Brazil, have received huge sums of money to wear popular brands of football boots. Corporate companies sponsor players to raise the profile and boost the sales of their brand of boots. Many players donate their used boots to charity or give them to club museums.

PATON'S
PROFESSIONAL
FOOTBALL BOOT LACES

PROFESSIONAL
FOOTBALL BOOT LACES
180 cms all cotton

England's Tom Finney promoted these boots

The modern look

The classic black-with-white-trim design, which is still used today, became popular in the 1950s. The vertical strap on the instep remains from earlier designs. The boots were becoming flexible enough to be worn without much breaking-in. There was less protection around the ankle, which allowed players more freedom of movement but led to an increase in injuries. It was at this time that bootmakers began to use the name of famous players to sell their boots.

The designer age

Huge sums of money are spent on the development of modern boots. Top-quality leather uppers, usually made from kangaroo hides, and light synthetic soles combine to make boots that last. They are comfortable and allow amazing amounts of spin on the ball. Former England captain David Beckham wore new boots for every single game. This pair featured the names of his sons.

Studs are screwed into the sole

Studs and stuff

The number and the position of studs on the sole varies greatly. Longer studs are needed for a wet and muddy pitch while shorter ones are worn on a hard pitch. Modern boots often feature studs of a fixed length moulded to the sole of the boot. The risk of studs causing injury concerns the game's governing bodies. The referee or an assistant must check the studs of everyone entering the field of play.

Nails fixed to studs

Separate nails

Key to tighten studs

Wooden hammer

The first studs

Early football boots were made entirely of leather. The studs had to be hammered into the soles.

Harmful hammers

Rubber studs came next. They also needed nailing to the sole and it was not long before the boots were damaged.

All change!

Modern screw-in studs are made of plastic or metal. Players can change studs at half-time.

Football kit

In the 19th century, both football and rugby players wore knee-length knickerbockers with no leg protection

A shirt, shorts, and socks were the basis of a footballer's outfit in the first laws of 1863. Players in hotter countries needed cool clothing, so wool gave way to cotton and then artificial fibres. Cool fabrics that "breathe" are now the norm worldwide. Teams wear matching outfits on the field of play in the club colours, which all the fans can identify.

Dutch orange

The orange strip for Holland is instantly recognizable. Dutch fans wear replica shirts to form an orange mass at matches. Here, striker Klaas-Jan Huntelaar wears the national kit.

Woolly jumpers

In the late 19th century, football jerseys were often made from wool. They stretched out of shape and became heavy during rain.

Away strip

In the 1966 World Cup final, the England team wore red instead of their usual white home strip. This was because West Germany were wearing white.

Lace-ups

At all levels of the game, teams began to wear matching strips. This black and white shirt was worn by a Newcastle United player at the 1908 English FA Cup final. Newcastle still wear black and white today. The shirt is made of thick cotton with a lace-up collar.

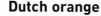

Australian amateurs

This wool Australian shirt with a cotton collar was worn in 1925 by Tommy Traynor. Shirts worn in international games have symbolic importance. After a game, teams swap shirts as a gesture of goodwill.

Keeping cool

Modern shirts are designed to keep players cool and draw away excess moisture. This 1994 Brazil World Cup shirt is made of light synthetic fabrics to suit today's high-energy games.

Fair-weather friends

By the early 20th century, manufacturers in many countries had begun to adapt the kit that British players had taken overseas with them in the 19th century. They produced lighter outfits more suited to warm climates. Short-sleeved shirts and deep V-neck collars became part of the typical Mediterranean look, as represented in this image from Valencia in Spain.

Early 1900s Spanish illustration

These socks are unusually decorative

Women were not expected to head the ball

Hoops and stripes are classic design features

Pull your socks up

These socks from the 1920s are made of wool. Modern socks are made of more comfortable synthetic materials. Players keep their socks up with ties around the top. Ties can be strips of bandage or elasticated tape cut into lengths. If players are prone to cramp, they may discard the tie-ups. Socks around the ankles can be a sign of a tired footballer facing defeat.

High kicking was easier if shorts were above the knees

Cream flannel shorts from about 1900

Hard-wearing cotton shorts from the 1930s

Modern synthetic shorts with decorative side seams

Early 20th-century French illustration

Under wraps

Until World War I, women footballers had to keep their hair under a cap or bonnet and hide their legs inside voluminous bloomers. In the 1910s, when many men were away at war, crowds flocked to see women's exhibition matches. This wider acceptance of ladies' football enabled women's teams to start wearing football outfits that were similar to those worn by men and more suitable for the game.

Short story

Amateurs in the 1860s played in full-length trousers but, as the game developed, players had to increase their speed and agility. Shorter knickerbockers cut just above the knee became popular. The baggy style of football shorts of the 1930s was made famous by Alex James of Arsenal, England, "the wee man in the big shorts".

Accessories

Injury and discomfort were part of football in its early days. This situation improved when protective equipment and other accessories such as hats, ear-muffs, and belts were introduced at the end of the 19th century. Shin-pads were developed in 1874 to protect players from injuries during games. Leg protection is still part of a player's kit, but other accessories are no longer used.

Lasting design

In the 1900s, players wore shin-pads like these outside their socks, held in place with straps and buckles. The front is leather, the back is cotton, and the stuffing in between is animal hair.

Buttoned tunic was an alternative to the more common shirt

Leather buckles fasten these shin-pads

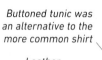

The first shin-pads

The earliest shin-pads were worn outside the socks and were extended to include ankle protectors, which rested on the top of the boot. Some, like these, had a suede covering, which was prone to water damage. These heavy and inflexible pads date from the 1890s, about 20 years after shin-pads became part of the footballer's kit.

Reinforced guards

This figure is from the box of a late 19th-century German football game. His shin-pads are strengthened with cane bars.

Early 20th-century schoolboys' belts

Belt up

Decorative belts were a part of many football kits until the 20th century. They smartened up appearances by holding in the shirt and gave teams identity through the use of colours.

Woman's belt from 1895

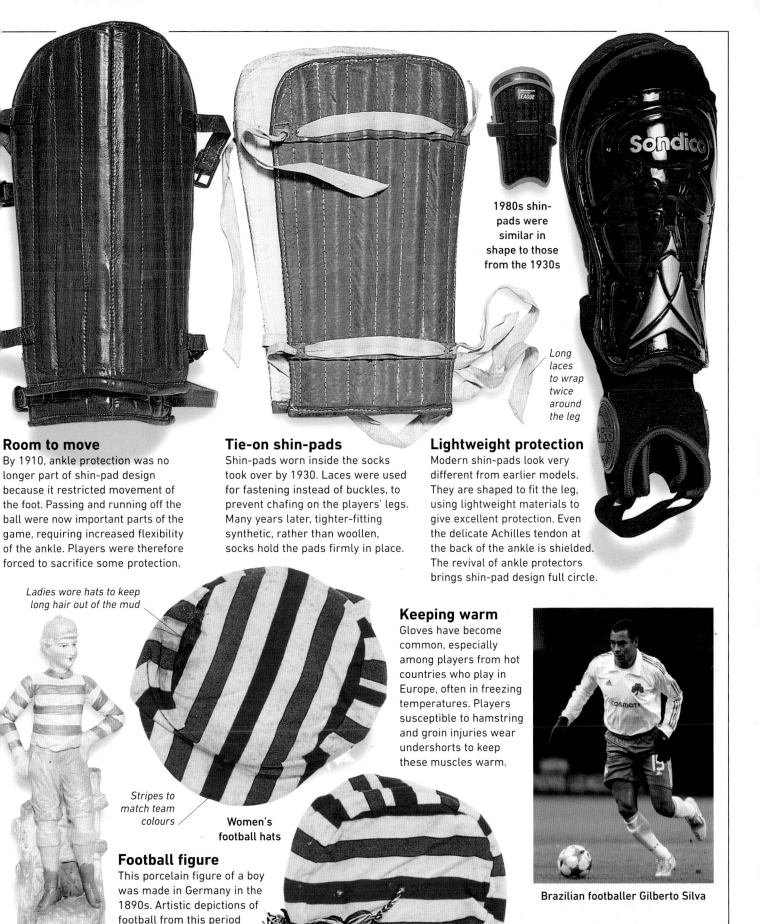

1980s shin-pads were similar in shape to those from the 1930s

Long laces to wrap twice around the leg

Room to move

By 1910, ankle protection was no longer part of shin-pad design because it restricted movement of the foot. Passing and running off the ball were now important parts of the game, requiring increased flexibility of the ankle. Players were therefore forced to sacrifice some protection.

Tie-on shin-pads

Shin-pads worn inside the socks took over by 1930. Laces were used for fastening instead of buckles, to prevent chafing on the players' legs. Many years later, tighter-fitting synthetic, rather than woollen, socks hold the pads firmly in place.

Lightweight protection

Modern shin-pads look very different from earlier models. They are shaped to fit the leg, using lightweight materials to give excellent protection. Even the delicate Achilles tendon at the back of the ankle is shielded. The revival of ankle protectors brings shin-pad design full circle.

Ladies wore hats to keep long hair out of the mud

Stripes to match team colours

Women's football hats

Keeping warm

Gloves have become common, especially among players from hot countries who play in Europe, often in freezing temperatures. Players susceptible to hamstring and groin injuries wear undershorts to keep these muscles warm.

Brazilian footballer Gilberto Silva

Football figure

This porcelain figure of a boy was made in Germany in the 1890s. Artistic depictions of football from this period often showed players wearing hats, even though they were becoming decorative rather than practical items.

Hand-painted German figure

Hats off!

These women's hats date from 1895, when ladies' football was still in its infancy. Like the men, many female players wore shin-pads for protection.

Famous players

Football is a team game. Clubs and national sides inspire the greatest passion among fans but a few players are so gifted and entertaining that they stand out and draw huge audiences. All of the great players share an ability to change the course of a match through a moment of incredible individual skill.

Gordon Banks (b. 1937)

English goalkeeper Gordon Banks is best known for a super save that kept out Pelé's header in the 1970 World Cup. Banks won 73 caps between 1963 and 1972.

Johann Cruyff (1947–2016)

One of the few great players to have become a successful manager, Cruyff instilled great tactical awareness. He played for Holland; Ajax, Amsterdam; and Barcelona, Spain. He also personified the idea of "total football" by floating all over the pitch using balance and skill to open up defences.

Gerd Muller (b. 1945)

Known as "Der Bomber", Gerd Muller was a springy centre-forward and a prolific goal scorer, with 68 goals in 62 games for West Germany. While playing club football for Bayern Munich, he scored a record 365 goals.

Milla was a great entertainer, known for his flamboyant goal celebrations

Roger Milla after scoring for Cameroon against Colombia in the 1990 World Cup

Roger Milla (b. 1952)

Twice African Player of the Year, Cameroon's Roger Milla was the first to become globally famous playing for an African nation. He was also the oldest player to appear and score in a World Cup match, in 1994, aged 42.

Bobby Charlton (b. 1937)

Manchester United star Bobby Charlton was known for powerful and accurate shooting, and proved invaluable in England's 1966 World Cup win. He was knighted in 1994.

Eusébio practises ball control in training

Eusébio scored 38 goals in 46 internationals

Diego Maradona (b. 1960)

Maradona was the best player of his generation. He inspired his team-mates, notably when leading Argentina to victory in the 1986 World Cup and Napoli to two Series A titles in Italy. His magical left foot and strength in possession were his main assets.

Maradona's low centre of gravity gave him excellent balance

In the 1986 World Cup against England, Maradona scored two goals – one a handball that should have been disallowed; the other a dazzling solo effort

Eusébio (1942–2014)

Although he was born in Mozambique, Eusébio was snapped up by Benfica of Lisbon, Portugal, and went on to play for Portugal. He starred in the 1962 European Cup final, scoring twice as Benfica beat Real Madrid, Spain, 5–3. Eusébio was respected all over the world for his fair play and dignity, as well as his footballing talent.

Meazza (below right) shakes hands with the Hungarian captain, Sarosi, before the 1938 World Cup final

Like many of the greatest players, Maradona liked to be number 10

Garrincha (1933–83)

Nicknamed "the Little Bird", Garrincha had polio as a child. He overcame his disability to become one of the quickest and most elusive wingers the game has seen. He played on the right-hand side of Brazil's legendary 1958 forward line. In 1962, he made up for the absence of the injured Pelé with some brilliant performances, helping Brazil to retain the World Cup.

Giuseppe Meazza (1910–79)

Italian Giuseppe Meazza won two World Cup winner's medals, in 1934 and 1938. He was a creator and scorer of goals from his inside-forward position. In 1938, he organized the Italian team when the coach was ordered to the stands. His best years were at Internazionale of Milan, Italy.

Maradona's magical footwork entertained and amazed the fans

Continued on next page **33**

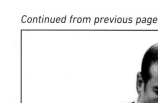

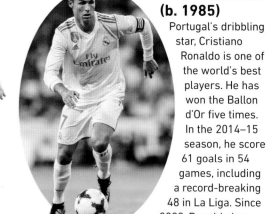

Lionel Messi (b. 1987)

A skilful forward, Lionel Messi made his competitive debut for Barcelona aged 16 and has since won eight Spanish league championships. The Argentina captain has won the FIFA Ballon d'Or a record five times.

Cristiano Ronaldo (b. 1985)

Portugal's dribbling star, Cristiano Ronaldo is one of the world's best players. He has won the Ballon d'Or five times. In the 2014–15 season, he scored 61 goals in 54 games, including a record-breaking 48 in La Liga. Since 2009, Ronaldo has played for Real Madrid.

Zidane combined balance with strength to provide a complete attacking threat

Messi's delicate touch and close control make him one of the world's best dribblers

Zinedine Zidane (b. 1972)

One of the greatest players of modern times, the French attacking midfielder Zinedine Zidane combined physical strength with skill and intelligence. In 1998, he propelled France to their first World Cup win, with two goals against Brazil in the final. He also helped Real Madrid to victory in the 2002 Champions League final with a man-of-the-match performance.

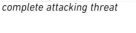

These two defenders are playing for the Italian club Roma

Roma defenders are left in Platini's wake

Stanley Matthews (1915–2000)

England's Stanley Matthews was known for his dribbling skills. He won 84 caps and played his last game for Stoke City at the age of 50. He was knighted in 1965.

Lev Yashin (1929–90)

Always in black, Lev Yashin played for the Soviet Union in four World Cups and is the only keeper to be named European Footballer of the Year.

Between them, Puskás and Di Stéfano scored seven goals in the European Cup final in 1960

Franz Beckenbauer (b. 1945)

Beckenbauer remains one of the few football-playing legends to achieve similar success as a manager. He captained West Germany to success at the 1974 World Cup, and managed them to the title in 1990.

Ferenc Puskás (1927–2006)

The star of Hungary's famous team of the 1950s, Puskás joined Real Madrid of Spain in 1958. Puskás favoured his left foot, scoring many goals for club and country.

Alfredo di Stéfano (1926–2014)

As Real Madrid led European football in the 1950s, Di Stéfano was a star player. He and Puskás had a legendary double act.

Michel Platini (b. 1955)

Platini captained France in the 1984 European Championships when they won the tournament for the first time. As an attacking midfielder, he often finished as top scorer at Italian club Juventus.

Michel Platini playing for Juventus

Platini had the speed and foresight to move forwards into space

Pelé (b. 1940)

Many people's choice of the greatest player of all, Pelé was king of Brazilian football from the late 1950s to the early 1970s. He scored more than 1,000 goals for Brazilian club Santos, American soccer team New York Cosmos, and Brazil. His enthusiasm and love of football make him a perfect role model for the game.

Winning feeling

Footballers lucky enough to win a championship are awarded a medal for their achievement. Those good enough to be picked to play for their country win a cap. Medals and caps have been part of the game since the 19th century and are still highly valued rewards today. Success can be measured by the number of caps a player has and passing the 100-cap mark is considered exceptional service to the national team.

Sew-on badge given to members of an international squad

Argentine pot made from a dried aubergine

Ornate silver dagger

Medals

As with military medals for soldiers, footballers are rewarded with medals for helping their side. Medals are awarded at all levels of football, professional and amateur. These mementos of glory days can become valuable collectors' items.

Good sport

Before organized leagues, football medals were often awarded for sportsmanship. The full-back C Duckworth was given this medal for "gentlemanly and successful play" in the 1883–84 season.

Norwegian silver spoon

Argentine silver spoon

With compliments

This "complimentary medal for defeating all comers" was awarded in the 1884–85 season.

Precious gifts

International players can receive gifts from opposing football associations. The England team received silver spoons from Norway in 1949. The Argentine FA gave the English team ceremonial daggers and other silverware on a visit to Wembley, England, in 1951.

Club strikers

Some clubs strike their own medals to mark a special achievement of their players. This medal was given at the end of a season to the team that won its league.

Lancashire Cup winners 1887

League 1889

FA Cup 1889

Double

These medals honour players from Preston North End who won the League and FA Cup in 1888–89, the first English "double".

Trophy triumph

This plaque marked a match between France and England in 1947. The English players received the plaque for victory.

Playoff prizes

Medals have been presented to the winners of the third and fourth place playoff match at every World Cup except 1930 and 1950. At the 2006 World Cup, host nation Germany's team won third-place medals.

Hungary hit

Hungary was quick to adopt the way other nations organized the game, including the awarding of medals. This medal was given to the members of an international side after a 1909 match against Austria.

1909 Hungarian medal

Champion

This medal was awarded to a player for success in the 1914–15 season.

Amateur

This 1920s medal was given to a successful amateur player.

Arsenal

This 1930s medal may belong to Arsenal football star Alex James.

Caps

A coloured cap was once the only way to know which team a player was on. In 1872, the FA ruled that teams should wear distinctive shirts. In 1886, it was suggested that caps be awarded to footballers each time they played for their country. Today, they are given to every member of a national team, including playing substitutes.

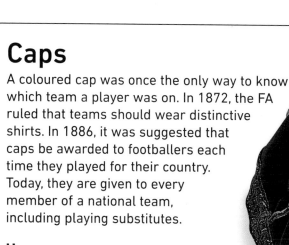

Tassels are added for decoration

Home cap
This Welsh cap was awarded for the 1903–04 Home International matches between England, Scotland, Northern Ireland, and Wales. This tournament took place every year until 1984.

Carey's cap
Defender Johnny Carey won this cap playing for Ireland in 1938. He won 36 caps.

Welsh national crest – a dragon

Details of matches can be embroidered into each panel

Football caps are often made from velvet

The date covers games from a whole season

Northern Ireland has had its own team since 1921

School colours
Football caps were first awarded in English public schools. "Colours", or caps, were given to the year's best players.

In training

Trainer Will Scott received this medal when the English and Scottish Leagues met at Celtic Park, Scotland, in 1931.

War games
Throughout World War II, famous international players took part in exhibition matches arranged to boost public morale. In 1946, Tom Finney was given this set of medals after a match in Belgium.

Promotional medal
By the 1950s, businesses commemorated football events. French newspaper *Le Soir* made this medal for a 1953 club tour.

World Cup
The biggest achievement in football is to win the World Cup. This Jules Rimet medal is from the 1954 final, when West Germany beat the favourites, Hungary.

Africa Cup of Nations
This medal was presented to the winners of the first Africa Cup of Nations. Sudan, Ethiopia, and Egypt took part. Egypt won the final 4–0.

Big clubs

Clubs inspire the greatest loyalty and passion from football fans. Big clubs in every country attract followers from beyond their local areas and usually dominate their domestic leagues and cups. Success for these clubs often continues because strong financial backing ensures a steady supply of good new players.

Bravo Benfica
Only Porto and Sporting Lisbon rival Benfica in the Portuguese League. Benfica were the great team of the early 1960s, winning two European Cups, in 1961 and 1962, and reaching but losing three further finals.

This bronze depicts Benfica's symbol, an eagle

The Old Lady
Juventus are the most successful Italian club and enjoy great support outside Turin. Nicknamed "The Old Lady" (*La Vecchia Signora*), they won the European Cup in 1985 and 1996.

Figure of the ancient Greek hero Ajax forms the basis of the Dutch club's crest

The club Ajax was formed in Amsterdam in 1900

Brilliant Barcelona
In 2015, Barcelona, inspired by their dynamic attacking trio of Lionel Messi, Luis Suárez, and Neymar, beat Juventus 3–1 in the Champions League final. It was the club's fourth Champions League victory in 10 years and sealed their reputation as one of the greatest club sides.

London ladies
Netty Honeyball was the force behind the first great women's team in the 1890s. The British Ladies Club drew large crowds for their exhibition matches in London.

Young talent
In the 1970s, Dutch club Ajax's policy to develop their own young players bore fruit. The players, including Johann Cruyff, helped Ajax to three consecutive European Cup wins in the 1970s. Despite regularly selling their best players, the club returned to the forefront of European football during the mid-1990s.

Busby babes

English club Manchester United started as Newton Heath before their name change in 1902. The Munich air disaster of 1958 killed eight members of manager Matt Busby's young team. The club have since won three European Cups.

Baines card from the 1890s shows Jack Powell

PLAY UP NEWTON HEATH

POWELL

Golden years

Bayern Munich followed Ajax to become the leading European team by the 1970s. They won three consecutive European Cups with players such as Franz Beckenbauer and Gerd Muller.

Paul Breitner of Bayern Munich in 1974

Dominguez, the goalkeeper – from Argentina

Alfredo di Stéfano, the leader of the team

Francisco Gento, the fast left winger

Real rivalry

In the late 1950s, Spanish club Real Madrid had legends such as Di Stéfano and Puskás inspiring them to win the first five European Cups. Real Madrid have a big rivalry with Barcelona.

The Red Devils

Here are Cagna and Rios of Independiente, Argentina, in 1995. Independiente were the first Argentine club to win the South American club competition, the Copa Libertadores, in 1964. The "Red Devils" won it four more times by 1975.

The fans

Gone bananas
In England in the late 1980s, there was a craze for taking large inflatables to matches. Fans waved bananas, fish, and fried eggs in the crowd to show their support for their teams.

Fans have made football the world's biggest game. From the late 19th century, working people began to have free time to attend sporting fixtures. They created an atmosphere of excitement and expectation. Today, football is the most widely watched sport in the world. Fans show their support for club and country in a range of noisy and colourful ways.

Preston North End, England, rosette

Manchester City, England, pennant

Holland scarf

Lazio, Italy, scarf

Perfect view
In their desperation to see a game, fans are not always put off by the "ground full" signs. In the 19th century, before large-scale stands were built, trees provided a convenient spot from which to watch a popular match.

Club colours
Colours are a vital part of the bond between a team and its supporters. Once, people made rosettes for big matches and displayed pennants. Now, fans often wear a scarf to show their loyalty.

Rare collection
Fans have always collected football-related objects. Today's items feature favourite clubs but past designs were general football scenes. Collecting autographs is also popular and offers the opportunity to meet star players.

John "Jack" Rowley, forward

John Aston, full-back

Johnny Carey, full-back

Matt Busby, manager

Child's money-box

1950s autograph book containing signatures of famous figures of Manchester United, England

Wooden pencil case

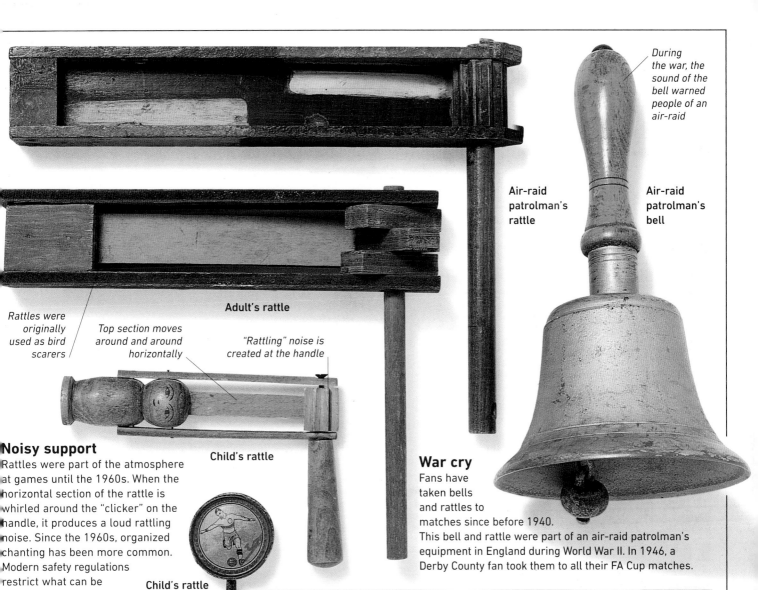

During the war, the sound of the bell warned people of an air-raid

Air-raid patrolman's rattle

Air-raid patrolman's bell

Rattles were originally used as bird scarers

Top section moves around and around horizontally

"Rattling" noise is created at the handle

Adult's rattle

Child's rattle

Noisy support

Rattles were part of the atmosphere at games until the 1960s. When the horizontal section of the rattle is whirled around the "clicker" on the handle, it produces a loud rattling noise. Since the 1960s, organized chanting has been more common. Modern safety regulations restrict what can be taken into stadiums.

Child's rattle painted with a football scene

War cry

Fans have taken bells and rattles to matches since before 1940. This bell and rattle were part of an air-raid patrolman's equipment in England during World War II. In 1946, a Derby County fan took them to all their FA Cup matches.

World beaters

Brazilian fans are famous for their noisy support. They produce a samba beat on the drums and blow their whistles. As the noise echoes around the stands, the fans dance to accompany the action on the pitch.

African painting

Face-painting in team colours is common at international matches. These two painted Zambian fans are at an Africa Cup of Nations match. Face-painting is most popular with Dutch, Danish, and Japanese fans.

Match day

This is a scoreboard from an early 20th-century French football game

The atmosphere of a big game, the sound of the crowd, and the closeness of the players combine to make live football matches so memorable. Football is now shown widely on television, but millions of fans still go to the matches. Many supporters, like players, are superstitious and follow the same match routines. Their noisy support is essential to the team's performance.

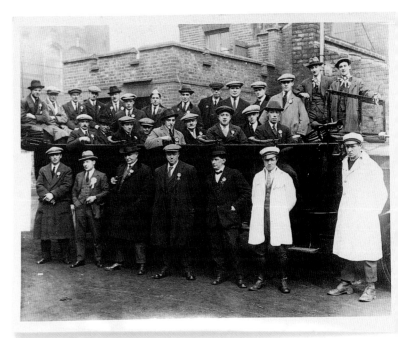

All dressed up
This photo shows fans of West Ham, England, preparing to travel to the 1923 FA Cup final, the first at Wembley. Many more than the official attendance of 123,000 crammed into the stadium.

In the 1988 European Championship final, Holland beat the Soviet Union 2–0

Holograms and complicated designs are now used to deter ticket forgeries

Tickets please
Tickets are essential in controlling access to games and keeping attendance to a safe level. Years ago, this was only necessary at cup finals and World Cup matches. Now that terraces have been phased out in favour of seating, each match ticket corresponds to a particular seat.

Reading matter
The earliest programmes were simple one-sheet items, giving team line-ups. Over time, further elements were added, such as a message from the manager and background information about the opposition. Glossy, full-colour brochures are now produced for all top-level matches.

Let me entertain you
To make matches more enjoyable, clubs and governing bodies lay on extra entertainment before kick-off and at half-time. In the past, this often took the form of brass bands. The opening ceremony at the World Cup finals in Germany in 2006 featured Bavarian drummers and dancers.

Major League fun

In the USA, there is a lot of razzmatazz at the Major League Soccer matches. Cheerleaders and music keep the crowds entertained. This is match day at Vancouver Whitecaps' stadium.

1903 FA official's badge

Official badge from 1905

The badges are made of cloth and decorated with gold brocade

FA badge from 1898

The English three lions motif

No access

Certain areas of the stadium, such as the boardroom, have strict access. These badges were sewn onto blazers worn by Football Association officials. Today, executive boxes are a feature of many grounds.

Badge worn at 1899 England v Scotland international

Crowd control

Police and stewards attend football matches to ensure spectator safety. Police, like these Italian officers at a Juventus match, may need to control unruly fans, and sometimes use horses or dogs to help in large crowds. They may also control traffic and escort supporters to and from the match.

Coming home

This drawing is from a 20th-century postcard. The caption on the card says, "Our team's lost by ..... goals to .....". Space is left on the card for fans to write the score. Sadness after defeat is replaced with fresh hope by the next game.

The stadium

Wembley towers
The famous towers at Wembley Stadium are sadly not part of the 21st-century stadium.

As crowds grew larger in the late 19th century, football clubs needed somewhere permanent to hold their matches. Stadiums became a necessity, giving fans shelter and a good view. A series of stadium disasters finally led to the belief that the terraces should be replaced by all-seater stands for the safety of spectators.

A new light
Floodlights were first used in 1879. The most common lighting was on pylons in the stadium corners. Today, lights are often placed in rows along the stand roof.

SHEFFIELD WEDNESDAY F.C.

Crowd safety
On 15 April 1989, the FA Cup semi-final at Hillsborough, Sheffield, resulted in the death of 96 Liverpool fans after a crowd crush. After the tragedy, there were new advances in stadium safety.

State of the art
The new Wembley Stadium in north London took much longer than anticipated to build and construction costs were considerably higher than initial estimates. Once it opened, however, the public flocked to this stunning stadium, with its 90,000 capacity and giant screens, each the size of 600 television sets. The stadium boasts a fantastic steel arch that is lit up at night and which can be seen right across the city.

Lights along the top of the roof

Standing taller
Barcelona, Spain, moved from Les Corts stadium to the spectacular Nou Camp in 1957. The Nou Camp was paid for by the club's members.

Path to the pitch
The tunnel is more than just a route on to the pitch. It is the place where players psych themselves up for the game, and many take the same place in line every time.

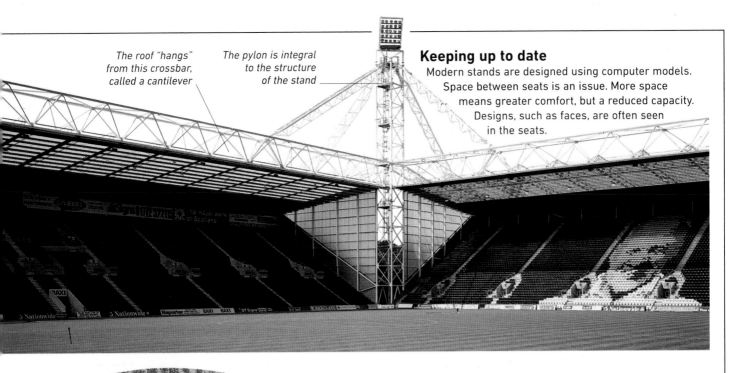

The roof "hangs" from this crossbar, called a cantilever

The pylon is integral to the structure of the stand

Keeping up to date

Modern stands are designed using computer models. Space between seats is an issue. More space means greater comfort, but a reduced capacity. Designs, such as faces, are often seen in the seats.

Fans on their feet

Before all-seater stadiums were introduced, fans stood packed on terraces. Far more fans could get in to watch a match and it is how most people have watched games in football's history. Children were often passed over the heads of the crowd to the front for a better view.

World Cup wonder

The Stade de France is in St Denis, north of Paris. It was built for the 1998 World Cup where 80,000 spectators watched the opening game between Brazil and Scotland. The stadium was praised for its dramatic design. The roof, enclosing the ground in a continuous curve, creates an amphitheatre effect.

Several tiers of seats

Pitch-level openings for emergency vehicles

Revolving advertising hoardings around the pitch

The World Cup

Football's World Cup is one of the greatest sporting events. The first World Cup was held in Uruguay in 1930. Some teams could not travel to the host country until the 1950s when travel became easier and quicker. As the tournament became more accessible, it grew in popularity. In 1958, Brazilian teenager Pelé became football's first superstar, and interest in the World Cup boomed.

Mascots
Every World Cup since 1966 has had a mascot. They feature as life-size figures and promotional merchandise. This is Pique, from Mexico '86.

World first
Uruguay offered to pay travel for the 13 visiting teams at the first World Cup. Four European teams made the long journey to join the South American teams.

1954 – Switzerland. West Germany beat Hungary 3–2 in one of the Cup's great upsets.

1958 – Sweden. Brazil beat Sweden 5–2. Brazil are the only team to play in every Cup finals.

1950 – Brazil. Uruguay beat Brazil 2–1, in the first tournament after World War II.

1962 – Chile. Brazil beat Czechoslovakia 3–1, with Garrincha taking centre stage after Pelé was injured.

1938 – France. Italy beat Hungary 4–2, inspired by inside-forward Meazza.

1934 – Italy. Czechoslovakia lost 1–2 to Italy. Uruguay did not defend their crown.

1966 – England. West Germany lost 2–4 to England, with Geoff Hurst scoring the first hat-trick in a final.

1930 – Uruguay. Uruguay beat Argentina 4–2, the first of many host countries to win the Cup.

1970 – Mexic One of the greatest teams ever Brazil bea Italy 4–1.

1974 – West Germany. Holland were beaten 2–1 by West Germany.

Venues
Many countries want to host this event to attract visitors. The 2002 finals, in Japan and South Korea, were the first shared tournament. Russia are the next hosts in 2018.

Argentina '78 is remembered for the ticker-tape in the River Plate Stadium

Mexico was the first country to host two finals

The Italia '90 mascot was called Ciao

1978 – Argentina. Holland lost 1–3 to Argentina, making the Dutch the best team never to win it.

1982 – Spain. Italy beat West Germany 3–1. Paolo Rossi was top scorer.

1986 – Mexico. Argentina beat West Germany 3–2, with Diego Maradona the star player.

1990 – Italy. West Germany beat Argentina 1–0 in a defensive, bad-tempered final.

1994 – USA. Brazil beat Italy 3–2 on penalties, winning their fourth Cup.

1998 – France. Brazil were well beaten 3–0 by France.

In 1994, American fans turned out in force to watch the matches

The fans at Italia '90 provided more drama than some games

The figure is a winged seraph

Top trophy

The first World Cup trophy was designed by French sculptor Abel Lafleur. First named "Victory", it was later named in honour of FIFA president, Jules Rimet. Brazil were given the trophy to keep in 1970, but it was stolen in 1983 and has not been seen since.

The trophy is made of solid gold

Sweden, the host team, made it to the final in 1958, but were overpowered by the Brazilian super-team

Read all about it

Programmes for the World Cup differ from the club variety because they cover the tournament rather than one match. They contain team information and are printed in several languages. These programmes are from Sweden '58, England '66, Spain '82, Italy '90, and USA '94.

This trophy's engraving is in French

COUPE DU MONDE DE FOOTBALL ASSOCIATION — COUPE JULES RIMET

Jules Rimet trophy

Didi

Pelé was 17 in 1958

Garrincha

Vava played at centre-forward

Zagalo, the left-winger, scored the fourth goal in the final

The beautiful game

The 1958 final saw Brazil become one of the World Cup's greatest teams. Their forward line-up was among the strongest ever. Mario Zagalo later became Brazil's manager and was in charge when they won in 1970 and 1994.

Continued on next page

We must have the World Cup
This was the poster for the 1962 finals in Chile. Earthquakes marred the run-up but the hosts were determined. President of the Chilean FA Carlos Dittborn said, "We have nothing. That is why we must have the World Cup." Chile overcame the doubts of some European teams by staging a successful event.

CAMPEONATO MUNDIAL DE FUTBOL
WORLD FOOTBALL CHAMPIONSHIP
CHAMPIONNAT MONDIAL DE FOOTBALL
COUPE JULES RIMET
CHILE 1962

World Cup Willie inspired a song by Lonnie Donegan

The Union Jack flag represents Great Britain

World Cup Willie was a lion, inspired by the three lions on the England kit

Mascots for money
World Cup Willie was the first World Cup mascot. Designed for the 1966 tournament in England, he represented increased commercialism. Mascots now appear on official merchandise.

Globe forms the top of the trophy

Designed by Italian Silvio Gazzaniga, the trophy is made of solid 18-carat gold

The real trophy is 36.5 cm (14.4 in) high and weighs 6.175 kg (13.6 lb)

New look Cup
The present World Cup trophy was made for the 1974 finals in West Germany. After winning for the third time in 1970, Brazil could keep the Jules Rimet trophy for good. The new trophy was commissioned by FIFA.

Replica of the World Cup trophy

Argentina '78

Thinking positive

In 1978, hosts Argentina inspired fans with their positive attitude. The star of their winning team was Mario Kempes.

Enthusiastic America

Despite having no strong tradition of professional football, the USA hosted a successful World Cup in 1994. Large and enthusiastic crowds attended the games. This is a ticket for the match between Italy and Mexico.

Spanish Football Federation crest

A pack of cards illustrating the stadiums

Hard work for hosts

Many countries bid to hold the World Cup years in advance. They try to convince FIFA that they can stage a successful tournament by producing information about the stadiums, transport networks, accommodation, and media facilities. Russia won the bid to host the tournament in 2018, while Qatar will host the 2022 event.

Who plays who?

Plastic balls are used to make the draw for the World Cup finals. It is a fair way to decide who plays whom. The number of competing teams has increased from 13 in 1930 to 32 in 2014. The present system ensures that every team plays three games in the first round. Games are then played on a knock-out basis, until only two remain.

Each ball contains a slip of paper with a team written on it

The balls are brightly coloured for the benefit of TV audiences

Zidane sees red

At the 2006 World Cup Final, referee Orazio Elizondo sent off French captain Zinédine Zidane after his head-butt of Italian defender Marco Matarazzi. With the score 0–0 after extra-time, Italy went on to win on penalties.

First for Africa

The distinctive sound of the vuvuzela horn was heard at the 2010 World Cup in South Africa. African teams have competed since 1970, but South Africa was the first country to host the competition. The 2022 tournament in Qatar will be the first to be held in the Middle East.

Top trophies

Olympic football

This badge is from the 1956 Olympic Games. The first proper Olympic football tournament was staged in 1908.

The moment when a team captain is presented with a trophy and holds it up to the fans is the crowning glory of any campaign. Cups and trophies are the marks of success and the managers of many modern clubs must win to keep their jobs. The desire to make money has led to the creation of many new competitions, some of which do not have the same prestige as older tournaments.

Team talk

First staged in 1956, the European Cup (Champions League) was originally for the champions of each country's league. Now up to four teams from a country compete. At the 1985 final at the Heysel Stadium in Belgium, 39 people died when a safety wall collapsed.

Programme for the 1985 European Cup final

Corner flags used as decoration

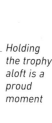

The gold-plated Women's World Cup trophy has a football at the top

Holding the trophy aloft is a proud moment

Full house

In the 1999 Women's World Cup held in the USA, teams played to capacity crowds. The final was held in the Rose Bowl in California. Here, US player Cindy Parlow rides a tackle in the final against China, which was won by the USA.

Early cup

This silver-plated trophy from the 1870s is an example of an early football cup. After the FA Cup was started in 1872, similar local tournaments began to be set up in England and Scotland.

Women's World Cup

The first Women's World Cup took place in China in 1991. The tournament grew bigger and drew large crowds. This is the trophy awarded to the USA in 1999.

Little tin idols

The first FA Cup, on the left, was known as the Little Tin Idol. It was stolen from a shop display in 1895 and never recovered. The present FA Cup, on the right, was made in Bradford, England, in 1911.

PLAYER'S CIGARETTES

PLAYER'S CIGARETTES

ASSOCIATION CUP WINNERS
THE OLD CUP

ASSOCIATION CUP WINNERS
THE PRESENT CUP

The silver UEFA trophy is decorated with men playing football

Names of previous winners engraved around the base

From strength to strength

The Africa Cup of Nations has been held since 1957. Although the first tournament featured only three nations, 24 teams now take part. Egypt captain Ahmed Hassan is seen here in 2008 after their 1–0 win.

The Copa América was conceived by Chile, Uruguay, Brazil, and Argentina

Copa América

First held in 1910, the Copa América is the oldest major international competition. It was originally for South American countries but Mexico and the USA have also taken part. Uruguay won the first official Copa América in 1917. Since 1987, the tournament has been held every two years.

Second best

The UEFA (Union of European Football Associations) Cup was originally known as the Inter City Fairs Cup. The first competition was played over three years, beginning in 1955. Barcelona beat London 8–2 in the two-legged final. When the European Cup-Winners' Cup was abolished in 1999, only two European club competitions remained. The strongest sides qualify for the European Cup and the next best play in the UEFA Cup. From 2009, the UEFA Cup became known as the Europa League and included a group stage similar to the one in the Champions League.

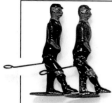

Two lead "kicking" figures from the early 20th century

Playing the game

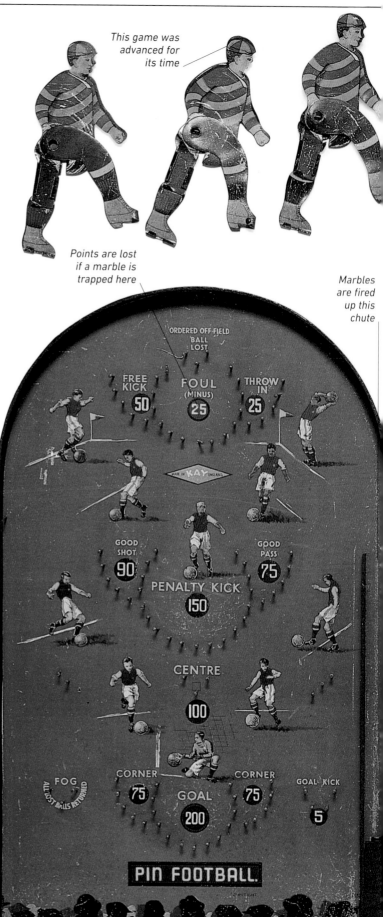

This game was advanced for its time

Generations of children had their first contact with football through toys such as blow football, card games, and Subbuteo. The popularity of football drives manufacturers and inventors to come up with new products, far more than any other sport. The simplicity of toys from the past contrasts sharply with the speed and excitement of modern computer games.

Points are lost if a marble is trapped here

Marbles are fired up this chute

Ball rolling

This hand-held toy from the early 20th century involves rolling the ball-bearing into one of the holes.

In the trenches

Trench Football was produced for British soldiers in World War I. The player must move a ball-bearing past the German generals to score.

Football matchbox

This is the world's smallest football game, probably made in Japan in the 1930s. As the matchbox opens, a spring is released and the players pop up.

Pinball

In this bagatelle game from the 1950s, players shoot marbles around the board using a spring in the corner. Points add up depending on where the marbles stop.

Ball for the
Kick game

Downward
pressure on
one leg causes
the other leg
to kick

The cards feature
various positions
and parts of
the match

Kick figures

These figures come from a
tabletop game called Kick,
made in about 1900. A green
cloth pitch and goals with
nets are included. Players
make the mechanical
footballers kick
by pressing them
down on the table.

Combination
of red and
white is
a classic
football strip

Key fits
into the
ball to
wind it up

Snap!

This pack of snap cards from the
early 20th century features football
characters. Players turn over
cards until two identical ones
turn up together. The first to
shout "Snap!" takes the cards.

Clockwork player

This tin-plate clockwork
toy was made in
Germany in the 1950s.
When wound up with
a key, the figure moves
forwards as if dribbling
the ball. The shirt is
typical of the kit worn
in Europe at that time.

Champions!

This game, called
Championship
Soccer, was made
in 1983. It uses two of
the classic components
of many board games –
dice and cards – to
govern the movement
of the ball around the
field. A scoreboard and
clock are also included.

Quick change

These wooden blocks
from 1895 have a different
picture on each side and
can be jumbled up to make
a character.

Memorabilia

Football can be used to promote a range of items. Football-related advertising and product promotion is nothing new. Companies were latching on to the game's popularity in the early 20th century. An understated style and original artwork dominated until the 1950s. This has been replaced by mass-produced items, reliant on star players and wealthy clubs.

1910 silver Vesta advertising the mustard maker Colman's

Bank Top White Star

PLAY UP WEDNESDAY.

SEE OTHER SIDE.

SCOTLAND ST. LAMBERTON HATTER

Wednesday, now Sheffield Wednesday

PLAY UP WALES

Welsh national team

CHADDERTON

Chadderton, a non-league team

HEART OF MIDLOTHIAN

Scottish club Hearts

Baines cards
These cards from the late 19th and early 20th century were the forerunners of sticker albums. They featured football and rugby league teams at professional and amateur level.

Sports tin
By the 1930s, original artwork on a sporting theme was often used as a decoration for household items. This tin features football on the lid and other sports on the outside.

Covered stands are rare in southern Europe

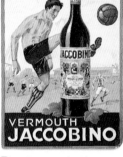

Poster painting
In this advertising card from the 1920s, an Italian drinks company has illustrated its product in a football scene.

VERMOUTH JACCOBINO

CORONA BRAND FOOTBALL STOUT THOMAS & EVANS LTD PORTH.

FOOTBALL CUP SPECIAL QUALITY

This label comes from a fruity soft drink. It was marketed as an ideal refreshment for half-time

This label implies that the drink will promote the robust strength that a footballer enjoys

ENGLAND ITALIA '90

ITALIA 90

FIFA logo for Italia '90

Souvenirs
Mementos of the World Cup finals do not stop at programmes and tickets. Many souvenirs are also popular, such as these erasers from Italia 1990.

Football fan
This Spanish lady's fan from the mid-20th century has a football image on one side and a promotional message on the back. Many commercial objects were designed to be artistic as well as functional.

Healthy kick
There is no magic football ingredient in this drink, but the manufacturers knew that any association with football would improve sales.

Banks Johnstone Jennings England Best

Team train

In the 1980s, the Hornby toy company of Liverpool, England, produced a series of these scale models of the London North Eastern Railway's locomotives, named after football clubs. This is the *Manchester United*. Real trains can be named after clubs.

Class B17 locomotive

Name plate

Petrol heads

The Cleveland Petrol company produced these miniatures of British international players in 1971.

The kicking leg is the second-hand

Pocket watch

Watch

Alarm clock

Chain

Full time

This group includes a Swiss pocket watch made in Geneva around 1910, a British watch from the 1950s, and a more modern 1970s alarm clock. Design, materials, and therefore cost, were dictated by whether the object was aimed at children or adults.

Chain medals

Football items are often turned into jewellery. Four silver medals from the 1920s are attached to this chain. The silver locket and compass are both from the 1880s.

Locket

Compass

Further medals could be added to the chain

Olympic clock

This German wooden clock may have been made to commemorate the 1936 Berlin Olympics. This football tournament was won by Italy, when they beat Austria 2–1 in the final. The figures at the top move on the hour.

The mould is made up of two parts

Chocolate

Melted chocolate would have been poured into this early 20th-century brass mould and left to cool and set, producing a miniature chocolate footballer with a ball at his feet. This item was made to appeal mainly to children.

Soap on a rope

The Avon company produced this soap football to mark the 1966 World Cup.

String along

Made in the 1880s, this copper string holder stops string from getting tangled.

The business of football

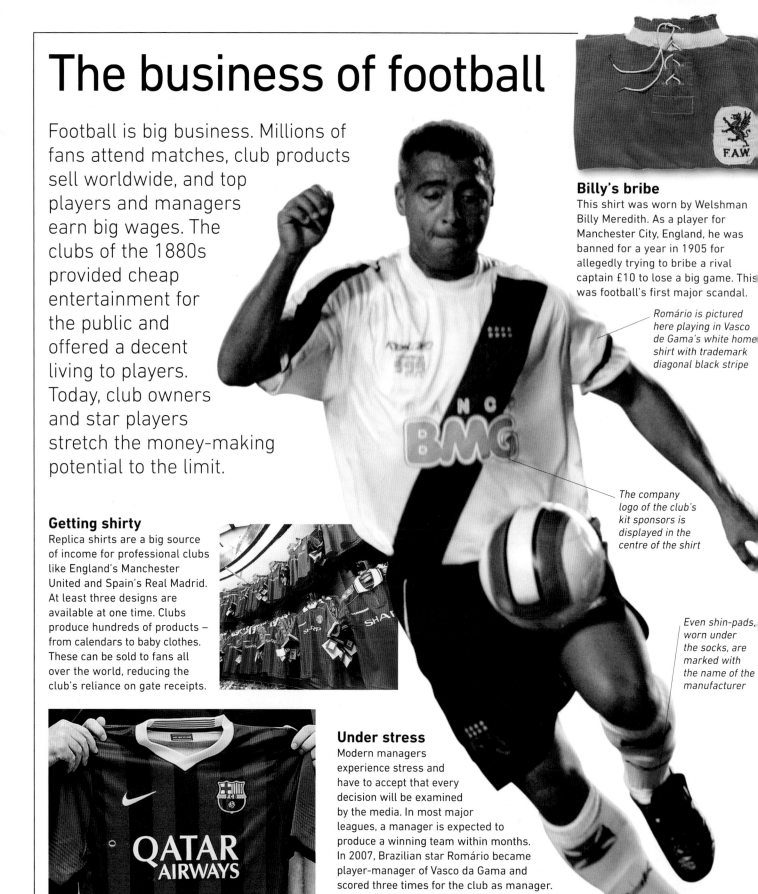

Football is big business. Millions of fans attend matches, club products sell worldwide, and top players and managers earn big wages. The clubs of the 1880s provided cheap entertainment for the public and offered a decent living to players. Today, club owners and star players stretch the money-making potential to the limit.

Getting shirty

Replica shirts are a big source of income for professional clubs like England's Manchester United and Spain's Real Madrid. At least three designs are available at one time. Clubs produce hundreds of products – from calendars to baby clothes. These can be sold to fans all over the world, reducing the club's reliance on gate receipts.

Shirt advert

Companies have been paying football clubs to put their logos on their shirts since the 1970s. But Barcelona only began a commercial relationship in 2010, resulting in sponsorship from Qatar Airways.

Under stress

Modern managers experience stress and have to accept that every decision will be examined by the media. In most major leagues, a manager is expected to produce a winning team within months. In 2007, Brazilian star Romário became player-manager of Vasco da Gama and scored three times for the club as manager.

Billy's bribe

This shirt was worn by Welshman Billy Meredith. As a player for Manchester City, England, he was banned for a year in 1905 for allegedly trying to bribe a rival captain £10 to lose a big game. This was football's first major scandal.

Romário is pictured here playing in Vasco de Gama's white home shirt with trademark diagonal black stripe

The company logo of the club's kit sponsors is displayed in the centre of the shirt

Even shin-pads, worn under the socks, are marked with the name of the manufacturer

Neymar's record

Players today change clubs regularly for the signing-on fees they receive. Prices have continued to rocket in recent years, with a new record set in 2017 by Brazil's Neymar. The superstar goalscorer became the most expensive player in football history when he moved from Barcelona to Paris Saint-Germain for £197 million.

Strikers, such as Neymar, fetch the highest prices

Ground force

Advertising in and around football grounds was allowed long before shirt sponsorship. In the 1950s, it featured mainly local firms, but now larger multinational companies exploit the exposure provided by television coverage. Some hoardings rotate to catch the eye of the watching public and allow more advertisers to use limited space. In some competitions, such as the European Champions League, the same products are advertised at every match in the tournament.

Badge showing AC Milan's club logo

World Club Cup

Media moguls

Italian media mogul Silvio Berlusconi bought AC Milan when television coverage of the game was increasing. He maximized commercial opportunities and attracted stars from abroad before he sold the club to a Chinese investment management company in 2016.

ll abroad!

olitical and legal hanges have made it asy for footballers to move abroad and play for oreign clubs. European nion (EU) residents can tay in any member state, while players from non-U countries must meet pecified criteria to play broad. Players from verseas, such as Ivorian nidfielder, Yaya Touré, re now in the majority t the Premiership lubs of England.

Ivory Coast's Yaya Touré has won the Premier League title twice with English side Manchester City

Europe versus South America

The Intercontinental Cup was contested by the top team in Europe and the top team in South America. Originally a home-and-away fixture won by the team with the highest aggregate score, it was changed to a single fixture in 1980 before being replaced by the World Club Cup in 2005.

The science of football

For many years, football was not a subject of scientific investigation, so coaches and players relied on knowledge from experience. As technology has advanced, science has made its mark on football. Nutritionists transformed players' diets, physicists studied how to bend the ball, and information technology has made a statistical analysis of the game.

Gender gap

In the past, women were marginalized for being physically unsuited to the game. However, as former Brazilian international Milene Domingues shows here, women have all the touch and skills of men, if not the bulk and strength.

Isotonic nutrition

Footballers can lose up to 3 litres (7 pints) of water during a game, so it is imperative that they rehydrate their bodies during and after a match. Isotonic drinks, which contain small amounts of salts and sugars, are the most effective at doing this. The drinks also help replenish the player's stock of calories.

German players exercise their abductor muscles, which lift the leg outwards from the body

The muscles in a player's leg have to learn to switch rapidly from relaxed to contracted and back again

Players run round poles to test their capacity to change direction at speed

With one foot off the ground, turning on the run, players develop their sense of balance

Training muscles

Training was once a few laps around the pitch, but advances in medical science have produced highly specialized regimes. Players warm up and warm down to avoid muscle strain and do specific work on muscle groups to cope with the range of moves.

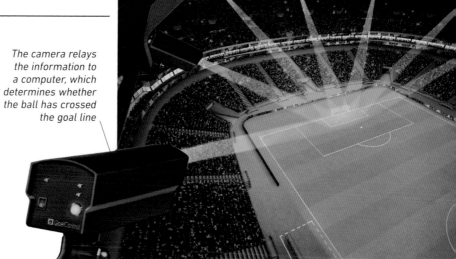

The camera relays the information to a computer, which determines whether the ball has crossed the goal line

Eyes in the sky

Did all of the ball cross all of the line? This is a question referees, players, and fans are always arguing over. New technology such as fast-frame cameras can now track a ball's movement in the goal area.

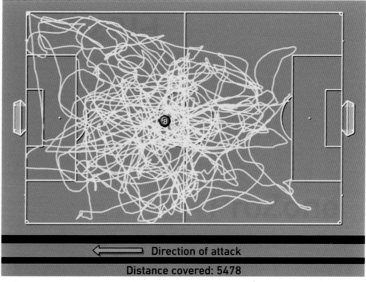

Direction of attack

Distance covered: 5478

Prozone

Software such as Prozone can track the movements of players in a game, recreate passages of play in animated form, and give statistics. This screen shows a central midfielder's movements. The dot in the centre is the average position, and the player has run more than 5 km (3 miles).

Bleeping flags

Assistant referees are now equipped with flags to attract the referee's attention. If something is missed, the assistant can press a button on the flag's handle. The referee's receiver, which is strapped to the arm, will then vibrate or bleep.

Flags with blip buttons like this were first introduced in the late 1990s

Physical demands

The German national team were put through their paces before the 2006 World Cup. Their levels of fitness were monitored and recorded in training exercises like this.

Did you know?

AMAZING FACTS

A three-minute egg

On average, each player in a match has the ball for only three minutes, the time it takes to boil an egg!

In 1965, substitutes were allowed for the first time, but only when a player was injured. Substitutes featured in the World Cup for the first time in 1970.

Luis Chilavert, goalkeeper for Paraguay, rushed out of his goal and scored for his team against Argentina in 1998. The final score was 1–1.

In 1974, Holland's Johan Neeskens was the first player to score a penalty in a World Cup final.

In the 1994 World Cup finals, Russia failed to qualify for the later stages even though they scored more goals in the first stage of the competition than any other team.

John Terry lifting the FA Cup for Chelsea after the 2009 final

Johann Cruyff's mother was a cleaner for the club Ajax in Holland. When she asked them to give her 10-year-old son a trial, they signed him as a youth player. He became an international star.

The goal net only became compulsory in 1892. The crossbar was introduced in 1875.

The first time teams used numbered shirts in an FA Cup final was in 1933. Everton wore numbers 1 to 11, and Manchester City wore numbers 12 to 22.

Eight of the players who won the World Cup for Brazil in 1958 were in the team that retained the World Cup in 1962.

Only eight different countries have been World Cup champions, although there have been 20 tournaments.

The FA Cup is football's oldest competition. The highest scoring FA Cup victory was in 1887 when Preston North End beat Hyde United 26–0 in the first round of the competition.

Pelé scored 1,283 goals during his senior career.

Half of the world's registered football players are from Asia. Japan's attacking midfielder Shinji Kagawa is one of the leading stars playing in Europe.

Shinji Kagawa playing for the German club Borussia Dortmund

After Brazil beat Italy 4–1 in the 1970 World Cup Final, reporters pursued Pelé into the changing rooms and interviewed him as he showered!

Uruguay, with a population of just three million, is the smallest nation to have won the World Cup.

The first international football match played by a side with 12 players was in 1952, between France and Northern Ireland. One of the French players was injured and substituted, but after treatment he kept playing, and no one noticed until half-time.

Two pairs of brothers, John and Mel Charles and Len and Ivor Allchurch, played in the Welsh team that beat Northern Ireland 3–2 in 1955.

QUESTIONS AND ANSWERS

Q Which is the most successful international women's team?

A By a small margin, the USA, which won the World Cup in 1991, 1999, and 2015. Germany has won two World Cups (2003, 2007) and hosted it in 2011. The USA were runners up once, in 2011, and have claimed Olympic gold four times – in 1996, 2004, 2008, and 2012.

Q Why was the first World Cup held in Uruguay?

A The other applicants (Hungary, Italy, Spain, the Netherlands, and Sweden) withdrew their bids.

Simone Laudehr of Germany

Q Were old footballs heavier than those used today?

A Old footballs were about the same weight, but today's footballs have a special coating to stop the leather from absorbing moisture and getting heavier.

Modern football

Q When were floodlights first used?

A The first recorded use of floodlights was at Bramall Lane, Sheffield, in 1878. The lamps were placed on wooden gantries and were powered by dynamos.

Q When were women banned from playing at FA clubs?

A In 1920, at least 53,000 fans packed into Goodison Park to watch Dick Kerr Ladies play St Helens Ladies. The FA, worried that the women's game was socially unacceptable, banned women from playing on FA club grounds in 1921. The ban was not lifted until 1970!

Q Which country was the first to be knocked out of a World Cup in a penalty shoot-out?

A Penalty shoot-outs were introduced at the World Cup finals in 1982 when West Germany knocked out France.

Q Who plays football in the Olympics?

A The national women's football teams compete in the Olympic Games, but for men only the national under-23 teams take part.

Q Who was England's first black professional footballer?

A Arthur Wharton, originally from Ghana, played for Preston North End as an amateur in the 1880s, and as a professional for Rotherham Town, Sheffield United, and Stockport County.

Q Why have there been four FA Cup trophies?

A The first trophy was stolen from a sports shop in Birmingham. When Manchester United won the FA Cup in 1909, they copied the trophy for a director. The FA withdrew this trophy and made a third FA Cup. Due to damage, this was replaced with a replica in 1991.

Q What has the phrase "back to square one" got to do with football?

A When the BBC first broadcast football live on radio in 1927, the *Radio Times* magazine printed a diagram of the pitch, divided into numbered squares. When the ball was passed back to the goalkeeper, the commentators said, "Back to square one".

BBC radio microphone

Record breakers

- Brazil is the only country to have played in the final stages of every World Cup.

- The oldest football club in the world is Sheffield FC. Formed in 1857, the club has always played non-league football.

- Lev Yashin (Russia) is the only goalkeeper to win European Footballer of the Year.

- In 1999, Manchester United made history by becoming the first team to win the Treble of the Premier League, the FA Cup, and the European Champions League.

- Real Madrid have won the European Champions League 12 times, more than any other team.

- In 1957, Stanley Matthews became the oldest footballer to play for England when he won his 84th international cap at the age of 42. He continued playing league football until he was 50 years old.

Stanley Matthews collector's card

S. MATTHEWS ENGLAND

Who's who?

Football is a game of speed and skill, with many outstanding players. In international competitions like the FIFA World Cup, extensive media coverage means footballers from around the world can become household names. Referees can also build up a global reputation. These pages contain some of the past and present players who are among the world's best.

Italian referee Pierluigi Collina

GOALKEEPERS

- **SEPP MAIER, WEST GERMANY, B.28.2.44**
The pinnacle of Maier's career came in 1974, when he won the European Cup with Bayern Munich, followed by the World Cup with West Germany. He played for Bayern Munich for 19 years.

- **PETER SHILTON, ENGLAND, B.18.9.49**
Renowned for his fitness and perfectionism, Shilton made his senior England debut aged 20. Over the next 21 years, he played for his country 125 times.

- **PETER SCHMEICHEL, DENMARK, B.18.11.63**
Schmeichel moved to Manchester United in 1991, where he won five league titles and two FA Cups. In his trademark "star" save, Schmeichel runs out, spreads his arms and legs wide, and jumps towards the striker.

- **GIANLUIGI BUFFON, ITALY, B.28.1.78**
A World Cup winner with Italy in 2006, Buffon became the world's most expensive goalkeeper in 2001 when Juventus paid Parma £32.6 million.

- **IKER CASILLAS, SPAIN, B.20.5.81**
Casillas made his debut for Spanish club Real Madrid in 1999 aged 17, and stayed there until 2015. He was captain of Spain for their 2010 World Cup and European Championship successes in 2008 and 2012.

Iker Casillas

DEFENDERS

Paolo Maldini

- **PAOLO MALDINI, ITALY, B.26.6.68**
Attacking full-back Maldini captained AC Milan and Italy, appearing for Italy over 120 times.

- **MARCEL DESAILLY, FRANCE, B.7.9.68**
Born in Accra, Ghana, Desailly moved to France as a child. In 1993 and 1994 he won the Champions League, with Marseille and then AC Milan. Desailly played a vital role in the French national team when they won the 1998 World Cup and the European Championship in 2000.

- **PAUL BREITNER, WEST GERMANY, B.5.9.51**
An adventurous, skilled left-back at Bayern Munich, Breitner moved forward to midfield on transferring to Real Madrid. He appeared relaxed and nerveless in big matches.

- **ROBERTO CARLOS DA SILVA, BRAZIL, B.10.4.73**
With a reputation for ferocious free-kicks, Roberto Carlos entered the Brazilian national team after the 1994 World Cup. A runner-up in 1998, he won the World Cup in 2002. He joined Real Madrid in 1996, winning the Spanish league in his first season.

- **SERGIO RAMOS, SPAIN, B.30.3.86**
A World Cup winner in 2010 and a two-time winner of the European Championships, Real Madrid's Ramos has been present for Spain since his debut in 2005.

- **FRANCO BARESI, ITALY, B.8.5.60**
The best sweeper in the world for much of the 1980s and 1990s, Baresi brought the ball forwards and joined in attacks. He retired in 1997, after playing more than 600 times for club team AC Milan during his 20-year career.

Bobby Moore

- **BOBBY MOORE, ENGLAND, B.12.4.41 – D.24.2.93**
A gifted defender and an excellent captain, Bobby Moore led England to victory in the 1966 World Cup. He played for England 108 times, only missing 10 matches between 1962 and 1972.

- **FABIO CANNAVARO, ITALY, B.13.9.73**
Although small, Cannavaro was a tenacious defender. He captained Italy to World Cup glory in 2006 and, the same year, became the first defender to win the FIFA World Player of the Year award.

MIDFIELDERS

• LUIS FILIPE MADEIRA CAEIRO FIGO, PORTUGAL, B.4.11.72
Figo was a European champion at under-16 level in 1989, and a World Youth Cup winner in 1991. He won the Portuguese Cup with Sporting Clube in 1995, and moved to Barcelona, where he captained them to the Spanish league title in 1998, before playing for Real Madrid.

• XAVI, SPAIN, B.25.1.80
An intelligent midfielder renowned for his incisive passing, Xavi was the heartbeat of Barcelona and Spain. He helped his club to four Champions League titles and his country to World Cup glory in 2010.

• ANDREA PIRLO, ITALY, B.19.5.79
One of the game's great passers, Pirlo enjoyed success at national and

Andrea Pirlo

international level. He won the Champions League with Milan twice, and the World Cup with Italy in 2006.

• FRANK RIJKAARD, HOLLAND, B.30.9.62
Rijkaard made his debut for Holland aged 19. A versatile footballer, he played midfield for Milan but central defence for Holland. He played for clubs in Holland, Portugal, Spain, and Italy.

• LUIS SUÁREZ, SPAIN, B.2.5.35
Considered one of Spain's greatest-ever players, Suárez dominated Barcelona's midfield in the 1950s and played a key role in the Inter Milan side of the 1960s.

• ANDRÉS INIESTA, SPAIN, B.11.5.84
A product of the famous Barcelona youth academy, Andrés Iniesta's ability to pass, shoot, and score marks him out as a complete attacking midfielder. He has won four Champions League titles with Barcelona, two European Championships, and one World Cup.

• SÓCRATES, BRAZIL, B.19.2.54 – D.4.12.2011
A footballer with tremendous poise, Sócrates made excellent passes and scored terrific goals. He qualified as a doctor before becoming a footballer, and returned to medicine when his career ended.

Sócrates

• LOTHAR MATTHAUS, GERMANY, B.21.3.61
An attacking midfielder with a thunderous shot, Matthaus played in five World Cup tournaments between 1982 and 1996, and has played in more World Cup matches (25) than any other player. He captained Germany to World Cup glory in 1990 and became the only German player to win the FIFA World Player of the Year award.

FORWARDS

• ROBERTO BAGGIO, ITALY, B.18.2.67
A gifted goalscorer, Baggio helped Juventus win the UEFA Cup in 1993 and the league title in 1995. He was FIFA's World Player of the Year and European Footballer of the Year for 1993.

• GEORGE BEST, NORTHERN IRELAND, B.22.5.46 – D.25.11.2005
An amazingly gifted player, Best had brilliant ball skills and balance. He was European Footballer of the Year in 1968.

• KENNY DALGLISH, SCOTLAND, B.4.3.51
Dalglish was probably Scotland's greatest-ever player. His ball-control skills could slice through a defence with bold, accurate passes.

• THIERRY HENRY, FRANCE, B.17.8.77
A striker with terrific ball control, incredible pace, and clinical finishing, Henry was top goalscorer for France when they won the World Cup in 1998.

George Best

• ROMÁRIO, BRAZIL, B.29.1.66
A prolific scorer at club level with both PSV Eindhoven and Barcelona, Romário also excelled at the international level. In 1994, his goals powered Brazil to a first World Cup title since 1970, and he was voted the world's best player at the end of the year.

• RONALDO LUIS NAZARIO, BRAZIL, B.22.9.76
Ronaldo scored his first goal for Brazil when he was only 16. An inspirational striker, his speed and skill could break through almost any defence. He was World Player of the Year in 1996, 1997, and 2002.

• ARTHUR FRIEDENREICH, BRAZIL, B.18.7.1892 – D.6.9.1969
Nicknamed "The Tiger", Friedenreich was a prolific striker blessed with a magical touch. He played in Brazil's first international in 1914.

Marco van Basten

• MARCO VAN BASTEN, NETHERLANDS, B.31.10.64
Goal machine van Basten was a three-time Ballon d'Or winner, won the European Cup twice with Milan, and took the Netherlands to victory at the 1988 European Championships. An ankle injury at age 28 made him retire.

• JOSEF BICAN, AUSTRIA/CZECHOSLOVAKIA, B.25.9.13 – D.12.12.2001
Bican was a prolific striker who represented the Austrian *Wunderteam* before World War II and Czechoslovakia after the war. However, he forged his reputation at club level: in a 27-year career, he scored 518 league goals – more than any other player in history.

63

World Cup wins

The World Cup began in 1930. By 2014, a global audience of 1.01 billion people tuned in to watch the final. The Cup's history is packed with super scorers, memorable moments, and amazing anecdotes.

WINNERS

Only eight countries have ever lifted the World Cup trophy:

🇧🇷	BRAZIL	1958, 1962, 1970, 1994, 2002
🇮🇹	ITALY	1934, 1938, 1982, 2006
🇩🇪	GERMANY	1954, 1974, 1990, 2014
🇦🇷	ARGENTINA	1978, 1986
🇺🇾	URUGUAY	1930, 1950
🏴	ENGLAND	1966
🇫🇷	FRANCE	1998
🇪🇸	SPAIN	2010

Italy lift the World Cup in 2006

HIGH SCORES

⚽ The highest score in the World Cup finals was when Hungary beat El Salvador 10–1 in 1982.

⚽ The highest score in a World Cup qualifier came in 2001, when Australia beat American Samoa 31–0.

IT'S A KNOCKOUT
At the World Cup finals of 1958, a Brazilian player called Vava scored against the Soviet Union. His team-mates mobbed him with such enthusiasm that he was left unconscious!

GREATEST GOALSCORERS

MIROSLAV KLOSE (GERMANY)
16 goals 2002–2014

RONALDO (BRAZIL)
15 goals 1994–2006

GERD MULLER (WEST GERMANY)
14 goals 1966–1974

JUST FONTAINE (FRANCE)
13 goals 1958

PELÉ (BRAZIL)
12 goals 1958–1970

JÜRGEN KLINSMANN (GERMANY)
11 goals 1990–1998

SANDOR KOCSIS (HUNGARY)
11 goals 1954

Brazil's Ronaldo

HAT-TRICK HEAVEN
When Brazil and Poland played in the 1938 World Cup, Brazil's Leônidas da Silva scored four goals. In response, Poland's Ernst Willimowski scored four more. Brazil's Romeo finally got the match-winner in extra-time.

YOUNGEST PLAYER
Brazil's Edu was 16 years and 11 months at the 1966 World Cup.

OLDEST PLAYER
Colombia's Faryd Mondragon was 43 at the 2014 World Cup.

FASTEST GOALS
AFTER KICK-OFF

HAKAN SUKUR	(TURKEY) v SOUTH KOREA 2002	11 seconds
VACLAV MASEK	(CZECHOSLOVAKIA) v MEXICO 1962	15 seconds
ERNST LEHNER	(GERMANY) v AUSTRIA 1934	25 seconds
BRYAN ROBSON	(ENGLAND) v FRANCE 1982	28 seconds
CLINT DEMPSEY	(USA) v GHANA 2014	29 seconds

STADIUMS

⚽ The first World Cup final, in Uruguay in 1930, was held in the Estadio Centenario in Montevideo. It had a capacity of just under 100,000 spectators, with many standing.

⚽ The final of the 2014 World Cup took place in the Estádio do Maracanã in Rio de Janeiro. One of the most recognizable stadiums in world football, the Maracanã was built for the 1950 World Cup. It is believed to have once held around 200,000 spectators but its current capacity is 78,000.

⚽ The 2018 World Cup will be held at 12 stadiums located all across Russia, from St Petersburg in the north of the country, to Sochi, 2,350 km (1,460 miles) to the south.

⚽ The capacity of the 12 Russian stadiums ranges from 42,000 spectators to 81,000. The opener and the final will take place in the Luzhniki Stadium in Moscow, the largest venue.

Estádio do Maracanã, Rio de Janeiro

TROPHY TRIVIA

NEW TROPHY

⚽ The existing World Cup trophy was first awarded in 1974. The name and year of every World Cup winner is added to the bottom of the trophy. In 2038, a new trophy will be needed because there will not be enough space left for new names.

⚽ The trophy is made of 18-carat gold! It is 36.5 cm (14.4 in) high and weighs 6.175 kg (13.6 lb).

OLD TROPHY

⚽ The original trophy was called the Jules Rimet Trophy in honour of the FIFA president from 1921 to 1954. The Frenchman set up the first World Cup finals in 1930.

⚽ The trophy was stolen twice. The first theft was in England in 1966, but a dog called Pickles later discovered it. The trophy was then stolen again in Rio de Janeiro in 1983 but never found.

GLOBAL AUDIENCE

The World Cup draws one of the largest audiences of any televised event on Earth and is viewed in private homes, public squares and stadiums, and even on mobile phone handsets. The 2014 World Cup in Brazil was broadcast in every country in the world and the final of the tournament is estimated to have been viewed by an audience of 1.01 billion.

ROYAL REQUEST

At the first World Cup held in Uruguay in 1930, the Romanian squad was handpicked by King Carol who organized time off work for the players!

BLANCO BOUNCE

The 1998 World Cup in France saw the introduction of a new footballing trick, courtesy of the Mexican player Cuauhtémoc Blanco. He broke through the defence by wedging the ball between his feet and jumping.

National teams

The beautiful game is played all over the world on streets, pitches, beaches, and in parks. In each country, the most gifted players join their national teams to compete in high-profile tournaments.

ARGENTINA

This South American country has a vibrant footballing history, with fanatical supporters and a packed trophy cabinet.

Argentinian Football Association founded: 1893
Nicknames: *Albicelestes* (White and Sky Blues)
Top goalscorer: Lionel Messi 58 (2005–present)
Most appearances: Javier Zanetti 143 (1994–2011)
Trophies: FIFA World Cup – 1978, 1986
Copa América – 1921, 1925, 1927, 1929, 1937, 1941, 1945, 1946, 1947, 1955, 1957, 1959 (round-robin league tournaments), 1991 (round-robin), 1993; Olympic gold medal – 2004, 2008

AUSTRALIA

After years of success in Oceania, Australia joined the competitive Asian Football Confederation in 2006.

Australian Soccer Association founded: 1961
Nicknames: Socceroos
Top goalscorer: Tim Cahill 48 (2004–present)
Most appearances: Mark Schwarzer 109 (1993–2013)
Trophies: OFC Nations Cup – 1980, 1996, 2000, 2004
AFC Asian Cup – 2015

BRAZIL

As the most successful footballing nation in history, Brazil has won the World Cup a record-breaking five times.

Brazilian Football Confederation founded: 1914
Nicknames: *A Selecao* (The Selected), *Canarinho* (Little Canary)
Top goalscorer: Pelé 77 (1957–71)
Most appearances: Cafu 142 (1990–2006)
Trophies: FIFA World Cup – 1958, 1962, 1970, 1994, 2002
Copa América – 1919, 1922, 1949, 1989, 1997, 1999, 2004, 2007

DENMARK

Denmark's highlight to date was Euro 1992 when the team caused a shock by beating West Germany in the final.

Danish Football Association founded: 1889
Top goalscorers: Poul "Tist" Nielsen (1910–25) and Jon Dahl Tomasson (1997–2010) 52
Most appearances: Peter Schmeichel 129 (1987–2001)
Trophies: UEFA European Championship – 1992
Confederations Cup – 1995

ENGLAND

Considered the founders of modern football, England's stand-out moment was in 1966 when the team won the World Cup.

Football Association founded: 1863
Nicknames: The Three Lions
Top goalscorer: Wayne Rooney 53 (2003–16)
Most appearances: Peter Shilton 125 (1970–90)
Trophies: FIFA World Cup – 1966

FRANCE

With a penchant for an attacking style of football, France is the epitome of entertainment.

French Federation of Football founded: 1919
Nicknames: *Les Bleus* (The Blues)
Top goalscorer: Thierry Henry 51 (1997–2010)
Most appearances: Lilian Thuram 142 (1994–2008)
Trophies: FIFA World Cup – 1998
UEFA European Championship – 1984, 2000
Olympic gold medal – 1984
FIFA Confederations Cup – 2001, 2003

GERMANY

Germany has an unrivalled record for consistency, reaching 13 major competitive finals and winning seven tournaments.

German Football Association founded: 1900
Nicknames: *Die Nationalelf* (The National Eleven)
Top goalscorer: Miroslav Klose 71 (2001–14)
Most appearances: Lothar Matthaus 150 (1980–2000)
Trophies: FIFA World Cup – 1954, 1974, 1990, 2014
UEFA European Championship – 1972, 1980, 1996
Olympic gold medal – 1976

ITALY

Italy has four World Cups to its name, and is the joint second most successful footballing nation along with Germany.

Italian Football Federation founded: 1898
Nicknames: *Azzurri* (Blues)
Top goalscorer: Luigi Riva 35 (1965–74)
Most appearances: Gianluigi Buffon 169 (1997–present)
Trophies: FIFA World Cup – 1934, 1938, 1982, 2006
UEFA European Championship – 1968
Olympic gold medal – 1936

IVORY COAST

The Ivory Coast reached the World Cup for the first time in 2006, and many of the nation's homegrown talents now play for great European clubs in their domestic leagues.

Ivory Coast Football Federation founded: 1960
Nicknames: *Les Éléphants* (The Elephants)
Top goalscorer: Didier Drogba 65 (2002–14)
Most appearances: Didier Zokora 123 (2000–14)
Trophies: Africa Cup of Nations – 1992, 2015

JAPAN

Football is now the second most popular sport in Japan, following four triumphs in the Asian Cup.

Japan Football Association founded: 1921
Nicknames: Samurai Blue
Top goalscorer: Kunishige Kamamoto 80 (1964–77)
Most appearances: Yasuhito Endo 152 (2002–15)
Trophies: AFC Asian Cup – 1992, 2000, 2004, 2011

RUSSIA

Although the nation has not won a major title for 50 years, Russia has established a strong basis for future success.

Russian Football Union founded: 1912
Top goalscorer: Aleksandr Kerzhakov 30 (2002–15)
Most appearances: Sergei Ignashevich 120 (2002–present)
Trophies: (competing as the USSR)
UEFA European Championship – 1960
(competing as Russia) None

REPUBLIC OF KOREA

The Republic of Korea co-hosted the World Cup finals in 2002. The nation drew international recognition by reaching the semi-finals, knocking out favourites Italy and Spain along the way.

Korea Football Association founded: 1928
Nicknames: Taeguk Warriors, The Reds, Red Devils
Top goalscorer: Cha Bum-Kun 58 (1972–86)
Most appearances: Hong Myung-Bo 135 (1990–2002)
Trophies: AFC Asian Cup – 1956, 1960

SOUTH AFRICA

After years of exile by FIFA for refusing to play a mixed-race team, South Africa was the first African nation to host the World Cup.

South African Football Association founded: 1991
Nicknames: *Bafana Bafana* (The Boys)
Top goalscorer: Benni McCarthy 32 (1997–2012)
Most appearances: Aaron Mokoena 107 (1999–2010)
Trophies: Africa Cup of Nations – 1996

SPAIN

Spain is realizing its potential thanks to victories in the 2008 and 2012 European Championship and at the 2010 World Cup.

Royal Spanish Football Federation founded: 1913
Nicknames: *La Furia Roja* (The Red Fury)
Top goalscorer: David Villa 59 (2005–14)
Most appearances: Iker Casillas 167 (2000–present)
Trophies: FIFA World Cup – 2010
UEFA European Championship – 1964, 2008, 2012
Olympic gold medal – 1992

MEXICO

A dominant force in the CONCACAF, boasting Latin brilliance on the ball, Mexico is becoming a contender on the global stage.

Mexican Football Federation founded: 1927
Top goalscorer: Javier Hernandez 48 (2009–present)
Most appearances: Claudio Suarez 177 (1992–2006)
Trophies: CONCACAF Championship and Gold Cup – 1965, 1971, 1977, 1993, 1996, 1998, 2003, 2009, 2011, 2015
Confederations Cup – 1999; Olympic gold medal – 2012

URUGUAY

Famous for being the first nation to lift the World Cup in 1930, Uruguay repeated this success 20 years later.

Uruguay Football Federation founded: 1900
Nicknames: *La Celeste* (The Sky Blue)
Top goalscorer: Luis Suárez 47 (2007–present)
Most appearances: Maxi Pereira 120 (2005–present)
Trophies: FIFA World Cup – 1930, 1950
Copa América – 1916, 1917, 1920, 1923, 1924, 1926, 1935, 1942, 1956, 1959, 1967, 1983, 1987, 1995, 2011
Olympic gold medal – 1924, 1928

NETHERLANDS

In the 1970s, the Dutch created "Total Football", a system in which every player could play in every position on the pitch.

Royal Netherlands Football Association founded: 1889
Nicknames: Clockwork Orange, The Orangemen, Flying Dutchmen
Top goalscorer: Robin van Persie 50 (2005–present)
Most appearances: Wesley Sneijder 131 (2003–present)
Trophies: UEFA European Championship – 1988

PORTUGAL

Long considered the underachievers of world football, Portugal finally won a tournament at the 2016 European Championship.

Portuguese Football Federation founded: 1914
Top goalscorer: Cristiano Ronaldo 75 (2003–present)
Most appearances: Cristiano Ronaldo 143 (2003–present)
Trophies: UEFA European Championship – 2016

USA

Interest in football rocketed when their country staged a hugely successful World Cup in 1994.

United States Soccer Federation founded: 1913
Nicknames: The Stars and Stripes, The Red, White, and Blue
Top goalscorer: Landon Donovan 57 (2000–14); Clint Dempsey 57 (2004–present)
Most appearances: Cobi Jones 164 (1992–2004)
Trophies: CONCACAF Gold Cup – 1991, 2002, 2005, 2007, 2013

Find out more

There are many ways of getting more involved in football. Find a club you want to support, and follow their match results. If you are keen to play yourself, join a team and take part in a local league. By visiting football museums you will find out about managers, coaches, and players. The more you learn, the more you will enjoy the football fever surrounding big competitions.

Match programme
Programmes are full of information about the teams that are playing, and are a great keepsake.

Bob Bishop was the Manchester United scout who discovered George Best, Sammy McIlroy, and many others in the 1960s and 1970s

USEFUL WEBSITES

- **To find out about the Football Association:** www.thefa.com
- **For information on the World Cup:** www.fifa.com
- **For information on English football clubs outside the Premier League:** www.football-league.co.uk
- **For up-to-date football information:** news.bbc.co.uk/sport/football
- **For playing tips and video masterclasses:** news.bbc.co.uk/sport1/hi/football/skills

Support your club
Choose the club you want to support and start following their results. If you can, go to some matches and start your own collection of programmes. Watching the matches and reading the programmes will soon make you an expert on your club's players and management. You will learn about football rules and develop your own ideas on team tactics.

Football scouts
All big clubs have scouts who travel around looking for new talent, from established footballers to buy, to gifted youth players. Outstanding young players are asked for a trial and may be invited to join the club's football academy where they receive an education and football training. If all goes well, they work through the youth and reserve sides to the first team.

Italian fans cheer on their team

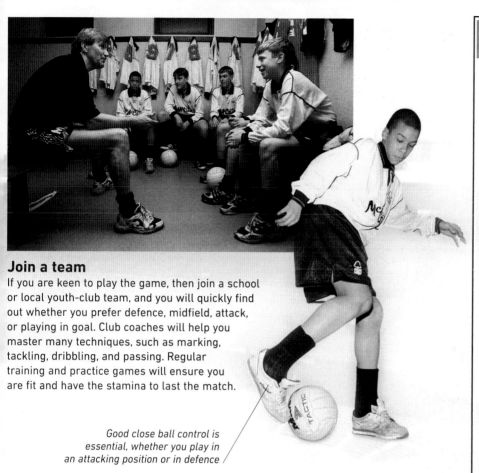

Join a team

If you are keen to play the game, then join a school or local youth-club team, and you will quickly find out whether you prefer defence, midfield, attack, or playing in goal. Club coaches will help you master many techniques, such as marking, tackling, dribbling, and passing. Regular training and practice games will ensure you are fit and have the stamina to last the match.

Good close ball control is essential, whether you play in an attacking position or in defence

PLACES TO VISIT

FIFA MUSEUM, ZURICH, SWITZERLAND
www.fifamuseum.com

This collection of historic documents, videos, and pictures tells the story of how football became the most popular sport.

THE NATIONAL FOOTBALL MUSEUM, URBIS BUILDING, CATHEDRAL GARDENS, MANCHESTER
www.nationalfootballmuseum.com

The world's largest football museum has the FIFA Museum Collection, and the FA and Football League collections. The museum holds more than 25,000 objects, 90 minutes of film and sound, and 1,000 photographs.

WEMBLEY STADIUM, WEMBLEY, LONDON
www.wembleystadium.com/Wembley-Tours/

A collection that includes memorabilia from England's World Cup victory in 1966.

THE SCOTTISH FOOTBALL MUSEUM, HAMPDEN PARK, GLASGOW
www.scottishfootballmuseum.org.uk

A collection of Scottish memorabilia.

LIVERPOOL FC MUSEUM, LIVERPOOL
www.liverpoolfc.com/history/tour-and-museum/home

Charts the history of Liverpool football club.

ARSENAL FC MUSEUM, HIGHBURY, LONDON
www.arsenal.com/emirates-stadium/arsenal-museum

A collection that highlights the achievements of Arsenal football club.

Players shake hands as a symbol of good sportsmanship

The 2014 FIFA World Cup

In 2014 the FIFA World Cup finals took place in Brazil. This was the 20th World Cup to be played, and the seventh tournament to be held in a Latin American country. As the host nation, Brazil qualified automatically, and were joined by 31 teams from around the world who got through via regional qualifying tournaments. Brazil was knocked out by Germany, who beat Argentina in the final.

Captain Billy Wright of England (right) shakes hands with Jean Baratte of France (left) in 1951

Glossary

AFRICA CUP OF NATIONS First staged in 1957. African national teams compete for the trophy every two years.

AGENT The person who acts on behalf of a footballer in the arrangement of a transfer or a new contract.

ASSISTANT REFEREES Formerly known as linesmen, one covers each side of the pitch. They signal offside, throw-ins, fouls, and substitutions.

BOOK The referee books players when they have committed an offence. He shows players a yellow card and writes their names in his black book. Players are sent off if they receive two yellow cards in one game.

CAP Originally a hat awarded to players in an international match. Players count their international appearances in caps.

COACH Runs the training programme, working closely with the manager.

COPA AMÉRICA First contested in 1910, South American national teams compete for the trophy every two years.

CORNER KICK Awarded when one of the defending team has put the ball out of play over the goal line.

CROSS A pass made from either wing to a forward at the centre of the pitch.

A referee's kit

DEAD-BALL KICK A kick from non-open play, such as a free kick or a corner kick.

DERBY A "derby match" is a game between two local rival teams.

DIRECT FREE KICK Awarded if a player kicks, trips, pushes, spits, or holds an opponent, or tackles the player rather than the ball. The person taking the free kick can shoot directly at goal.

DIRECTORS The people who serve on a board to help run a club. Some put a lot of personal money into the club.

DRIBBLING Running with the ball while keeping it under close control.

EUROPEAN CUP First contested in 1956, it is now known as the Champions League. The top clubs from the league of each European country compete for the trophy every year.

FA CUP First contested in 1872. English league and non-league teams compete annually for the trophy.

FIFA (FÉDÉRATION INTERNATIONALE DE FOOTBALL ASSOCIATION) Formed in 1904, the world governing body of football, FIFA, arbitrates between countries, and runs the World Cup and the Women's World Cup.

FOOTBALL ASSOCIATION Formed in 1863, the national governing body arbitrates between clubs and disciplines players.

Using your chest to control the ball

FORMATION The arrangement of the players on the pitch. The coach or manager chooses the formation, and may change it during a game in response to the strengths or weaknesses of the opposition.

GIANT KILLER A team that beats a side believed to be of a much higher quality, and from a higher division.

GLOVES Worn by goalkeepers to protect their hands and to help them grip the ball.

GOAL KICK Awarded when the ball goes out of play over the goal line if it was last touched by the attacking team.

GROUND STAFF The people who look after the stadium, the terraces, and the football pitch.

HANDBALL It is an offence to touch the ball with your hands or arms during play.

HEADING A defensive header sends the ball upwards, clearing it as far away as possible. An attacking header sends the ball downwards, hopefully into the goal.

INDIRECT FREE KICK Awarded when a team commits an offence other than a foul, such as obstruction. The player cannot score directly.

The white ball was introduced in 1951

KICK-OFF The kicking of the ball from the centre spot to start the game.

LAWS The 17 Laws of the Game approved by FIFA.

MANAGER The person who picks the team, plans tactics, motivates the players, and decides what to do in training.

MARKING Staying close to an opponent to prevent him or her from passing, shooting, or receiving the ball.

MASCOT A person, animal, or doll that is considered to bring good luck to a team. Mascots are also part of the increasing commercialization of football.

OFFSIDE When an attacking player receives a ball, two defenders including the goalkeeper have to be between the attacking player and the goal. Players are only penalized for being offside if they interfere with play or gain some advantage by being in that position.

ONE-TWO An attacking player passes the ball to an advanced team-mate, and runs on into a space. The ball is immediately returned, bypassing the defending player.

PENALTY AREA A box that stretches 18 yd (16.5 m) in front of and to either side of the goal.

PENALTY KICK A shot at goal from the penalty spot. Awarded against a team that commits an offence in its own penalty area.

PENALTY SPOT The spot 14 yd (13 m) in front of the goal. The ball is placed here to take a penalty.

PHYSIOTHERAPIST The person who helps players recover from injuries, and who checks players to ensure that they are fit enough for a match.

PITCH The field of play. In the early days, the boundaries of the pitch were marked by a series of flags. The FA introduced the pitch markings we know today in 1902.

PROGRAMME Provides information for the fans about the players of their team and of the opposition, as well as a message from the manager.

RATTLE Supporters took rattles into matches until the 1960s, when they started to sing or chant instead. These rattles are now forbidden.

RED CARD The referee holds up a red card to show that a player has to leave the pitch. Serious foul play or two bookable offences results in a red card.

REFEREE The person who has the authority to enforce the Laws of the Game.

SCARF Each team has a scarf in its own colours. Fans often wear the scarf or their team's strip when they go to matches.

SCOUT A person employed by a club to look for talented new players.

SET-PIECE Moves practised by a team to take advantage of a dead-ball situation.

PLAYER'S CIGARETTES

KICKING TO SWERVE THE BALL

A football card

SHIN-PADS Pads worn inside socks to protect the lower legs.

SHOOTING A kick towards the goal.

STANDS The areas where the supporters sit around the pitch.

STRIP The shirt, shorts, and socks a team wears. Most clubs have at least two different strips, a home kit and an away kit. A team uses its away kit when there is a conflict of colours.

STUDS Small, rounded projections screwed into the sole of a football boot. The referee or assistant referee checks all studs before play starts. Players use longer studs on a wet, muddy pitch.

SUPERSTITIONS Many players are deeply superstitious. For example, they may insist on wearing the same shirt number throughout their career. England footballer Paul Ince would only put his shirt on for a match when running out of the tunnel.

TACKLING Stopping an opponent who has the ball and removing the ball with your feet.

TACTICS Planned actions or movements to gain an advantage over your opponents.

TERRACES Steps where people stood to watch a match before the advent of all-seater stadiums.

THROW-IN A way of restarting play when the ball goes over the touchline. Awarded to the opponent of the player who last touched the ball.

World Cup medal

UEFA EUROPA LEAGUE Originally known as the Inter City Fairs Cup, it was first contested in 1958. It changed its name to UEFA Cup and was renamed UEFA Europa League in 2009–10. Some of the best teams from each European country's national league compete for the trophy every year.

WARM-UP A routine of exercises to warm up all the muscles before the start of a match.

WHISTLE Used by the referee at the beginning and end of a match and to stop play when there is a foul.

WINGER A striker who plays particularly on one side of the pitch or the other.

WOMEN'S WORLD CUP First contested in 1991. National women's teams compete for the trophy every four years.

WORLD CUP First contested in 1930. National men's teams compete for the trophy every four years.

YELLOW CARD The referee holds up a yellow card to book a player.

The USA women's football team, 2011

Index

Acknowledgments

Dorling Kindersley would like to thank Hugh Hornby, Rob Pratten, Lynsey Jones, & Mark Bushell at The National Football Museum for their help and patience; Stewart J Wild for proofreading; Helen Peters for the index; David Ekholm-JAlbum, Sunita Gahir, David Goldblatt, Susan St Louis, Lisa Stock, & Bulent Yusuf for the clipart; Neville Graham, Sue Nicholson, Susan St Louis for the wallchart; Andrea Mills for editing and Victoria Pyke for proofreading the relaunch edition.

The publishers would also like to thank the following for their kind permission to reproduce their photographs:
a=above; c=centre; b=below; l=left; r=right; t=top; f=far; n=near

123RF.com: bagwold / "adidas, the 3-Bars logo, BRAZUCA and the Brazuca ball design are registered trademarks of adidas, used with permission." 2clb. **Action Images:** 31crb; Toby Melville / Reuters 27cra; Bruno Domingos / Reuters 56r; Sporting Images 23c; Sporting Pictures 22c. **Action Plus:** Glyn Kirk 56c; Neil Tingle 10fbr, 60-61 (background), 68b. **Alamy:** Brent Clark 63cla; wareham.nl 71b; **Colorsport:** 11tr, 21br, 32clb, 39tr, 44-45, 57tr, 68tl; Olympia 35cr, 35tr; Jerome Provost 39bc. **Corbis:** Ben Queenborough / BPI 57bc; Chen Shaojin / Xinhua Press 17bl; Christian Liewig / Liewig Media Sports 16clb; Frans Lanting 65tc; Matthew Ashton / AMA / Corbis Sports 34tc, 60cb, 65cr; S Carmona 44clb; Stephane Reix / Photo & Co. 34tl; Stephane Reix / Corbis Sports 66-67 (background); Tolga Bozoglu / Epa 62bc; Universal / TempSport 69br; Visionhaus 27tr. **Dorling Kindersley:** Football Museum, Preston / 1974 FIFA TM 48r; Football Museum, Preston / Adidas 18br; Football Museum, Preston / FIFA 46fbr (1998), 49fcr; Football Museum, Preston / Sondico 31ftr; Football Museum, Preston / Umbro 28br; Football Museum, Preston 1, 2cb, 2c, 2r, 2cla (rubber tube), 2cl, 2fbl, 2fcl, 2ftl (brass pump), 2ftr, 2tc, 2tl (gauged pump), 3c, 3ftl, 3ftr, 4bc, 4bl, 4br (pin), 4cla, 4crb, 4fbl, 4fbr (ball), 4fbr (boot), 4tl, 4tr, 5br, 5fbr, 5ftl, 5ftr (Brazil), 5ftr (Italy), 5tl, 5tr (Dutch), 5tr (Hungary), 6b, 6c, 6fcra, 6tr, 7bc, 7cb, 7crb, 7l, 7tr, 8c, 8ca, 8fbr, 8ftr, 8l, 8tr, 9br, 9cr, 9crb, 9fclb, 9l, 9tr, 10clb, 10fclb, 10tl, 10-11, 12br, 12cb (whistle), 12fclb, 12tl, 13br, 13cr, 13ftr (Bangladesh), 13ftr (Columbia), 13ftr (Italy), 13ftr (New Zealand), 13ftr (USA), 13tr (Australia), 13tr (Iceland), 13tr (Portugal), 13tr (USSR), 14br, 14ca, 14tl, 15bl, 15cl, 15clb, 15clb (side view), 15cr, 16tl, 17br, 18bl, 18cb, 18cr, 18tl, 18tr, 19bl, 19tl, 20bl, 20tl, 20tr, 21bl, 21cra, 21crb, 21tr, 22cla, 22tl, 22tr, 22-23, 24bc, 24cl, 24crb, 24ftl, 24tr, 25bl, 25cb, 25crb, 25ftl (brass), 25ftl (gauged pump), 25ftr, 25tl (pump), 25tl (rubber), 25tr, 26br, 26cl, 26cr, 26fcr, 26tl, 26tr, 27bc (hammer), 27bc (studs), 27br (nails), 27br (studs), 27c, 27cla, 27fbr (key), 27fbr (studs), 27fbr (wrench), 27tl, 28bl, 28crb, 28tl, 29bl; 29cr, 29tl, 29tr, 30br, 30c, 30cl, 30crb, 30tl, 30tr, 31bc, 31bl, 31clb, 31tc, 31tl, 31tr, 36bc, 36c, 36cb, 36cl, 36clb, 36cra, 36fbr, 36fcl, 36fcrb, 36ftl, 36ftr, 36tr, 36tr (spoon), 37bl, 37br, 37c, 37cb, 37cr, 37fbl, 37fcrb, 37tr, 38bl, 38br, 38tl, 38-39, 39cr, 39tl, 40b, 40ca, 40cb, 40cl, 40crb, 40ftl, 40ftr, 40tr, 41ca, 41cl, 41clb, 41tr, 42cr, 42tl, 42tr, 43br, 43cra, 43fcr, 43ftr, 43tr, 44ftr, 44tl, 44tr, 45cl, 45tr, 46bc (1986), 46bl (1978), 46bl (1982), 46br (1990), 46br (1994), 46c (1954), 46c (1958), 46cl (1938), 46cl (1950), 46clb (1930), 46clb (1934), 46cr (1962), 46fcr (1966), 46fcrb (1970), 46fcrb (1974), 46tl, 46tr, 47br, 47tr, 48bl, 48tl, 49ftl, 49tl, 49tr, 50cl, 50tl, 50tr, 51tl, 52br, 52c, 52fbl, 52fcl, 52ftl, 52-53, 53bc, 53bl, 53cla, 53cr, 56tr, 57crb, 61tr, 70tc, 71cla; Mark Leech 43bl; The Science Museum, London 61tr. **Dreamstime.com:** Alexander Lebedev 12tr; Greg Da Silva 49br; Kampee Patisena 20crb; Zedcreations 20crb (iPad). **Getty Images:** 62cr, 63tr; AFP Photo / Pierre-Philippe Marcou 58tl; AFP Photo / Roberto Schmidt 50c; AFP Photo DDP / Thomas Lohnes 58b; Allsport 34-35; Allsport / Hulton Archive 34bl; Allsport / Vincent Laforet 50br; Lars Baron / Bongarts 16cl; Shaun Botterill 62-63 (background); Shaun Botterill / Getty Images Sport 64-65; Clive Brunskill 14bl; David Cannon / Allsport 33c, 51r; David Cannon / Getty Images Sport 23tl, 64cl; Central Press / Hulton Archive 32cla, 33cr; Mark Cosgrove 10crb; Jean Catuffe 57tl; Tom Dulat 15t; Tony Duffy / Allsport 32br; Mike Hewitt / FIFA 2r; Stuart Franklin / Bongarts 59bc; Gallo Images / Getty Images Sport 51cl; Markus Gilliar - Pool / Bongarts 58-59; Scott Heavey 61tl; Patrick Hertzog / AFP 65br; Mike Hewitt 42br; Mike Hewitt / Getty Images Sport 19c; Jasper Juinen / Getty Images Sport 16r; Jeff Vinnick 43tl; Keystone / Hulton Archive 33bl, 33tl; Ross Kinnaird 58c; David Leah 51c; John Macdougall / AFP / 2005 FIFA TM 69clb; Josep Lago / AFP 56bl; Clive Mason 17tl; Damien Meyer / AFP 13l; Paolo Nucci / WireImage 49bl; NurPhoto 2c; Doug Pensinger / Getty Images Sport 17c; Popperfoto.com 68cl; Power Sport Images 34cra; Gary M. Prior 62tr; Michael Urban / AFP 36bl; VI-Images 38cl; Dave Winter 21c. **Bryan Hornsell:** 42c, 42cl, 42fcl. **Press Association Images:** AP Photo / Lewis Whyld 44cla; Matthew Ashton / Empics Ltd 68-69 (background); Matthew Ashton / Empics Sport 16tr; Jon Buckle / Empics Ltd 70-71 (background); Adam Davy / Empics Sport 62c; Empics Ltd 32tr; Alastair Grant / Associated Press 71tr; Laurence Griffiths / Empics Ltd 69ca, 69tl; Tony Marshall / Empics Sport 28tr; PA Archive 34bc; Peter Robinson 63bl; Peter Robinson / Empics 47l; Peter Robinson / Empics Sport 57fcrb; Michael Steele / Empics Sport 41br, 41fclb; Topham Picturepoint 35tl; Witters 32fbl. **Rex Shutterstock:** Colorsport 63cra. **Wallchart:** Colorsport: cla, cl (Arthur Rowe). **Corbis:** Franck Seguin cb. **Dorling Kindersley:** Football Museum, Preston tl (Chinese characters), ftl (Lord Kinnaird), cra, crb, tr. **Dreamstime.com:** Pumba1 bl. **Getty Images:** © 1974 FIFA™ / David Leah / Mexsport crb, Time & Life Pictures ca (Pele); AFP Photo / Pierre-Philippe Marcou br. **iStockphoto.com:** sdominick clb. **Nike:** clb/ (Boots)

All other images © Dorling Kindersley
For further information see:
www.dkimages.com